Minimalist Living:
2 Books in 1:
Declutter Your Mind + Minimalist Budget using Minimalism Essentials to Declutter, Organize and Simplify Your Life

*Declutter Your Mind:
How to Free Your Thoughts from Worry, Anxiety & Stress using Mindfulness Techniques for Better Mental Clarity and to Simplify Your Life*

*Minimalist Budget:
Simple and Practical Budgeting Strategies to Save Money, Avoid Compulsive Spending, Pay Off Debt and Simplify Your Life*

Marie S. Davenport

About this Bundle:

Congratulations on owning ***Minimalist Living: 2 Books in 1: Declutter Your Mind + Minimalist Budget using Minimalism Essentials to Declutter, Organize and Simplify Your Life***, and thanks for doing so.

What you are about to read is a collection of two separate books on Minimalist Living that would benefit you as someone who wants to experience living more with less. The first book will be about decluttering your mind while the second book will discuss minimalist budgeting.

Book 1:
[Declutter Your Mind: How to Free Your Thoughts from Worry, Anxiety & Stress using Mindfulness Techniques for Better Mental Clarity and to Simplify Your Life](#)

Here you will learn how to free yourself from mental clutter by teaching you mental declutter techniques.

Book 2:
[Minimalist Budget: Simple and Practical Budgeting Strategies to Save Money, Avoid Compulsive Spending, Pay Off Debt and Simplify Your Life](#)

Here you will learn the best methods for budgeting and applying minimalism for simple living and achieving your personal finance goals.

Thanks again for owning this book!

Let us begin with the first book in the Minimalist Living bundle:

Declutter Your Mind:

How to Free Your Thoughts from Worry, Anxiety & Stress using Mindfulness Techniques for Better Mental Clarity and to Simplify Your Life

Marie S. Davenport

© **Copyright 2018 by Marie S. Davenport - All rights reserved.**

The contents of this book may not be reproduced, duplicated or transmitted without direct written permission from the author.

Under no circumstances will any legal responsibility or blame be held against the publisher for any reparation, damages, or monetary loss due to the information herein, either directly or indirectly.

Legal Notice:

This book is copyright protected. This is only for personal use. You cannot amend, distribute, sell, use, quote or paraphrase any part or the content within this book without the consent of the author.

Disclaimer Notice:

Please note the information contained within this document is for educational and entertainment purposes only. Every attempt has been made to provide accurate, up to date and reliable complete information. No warranties of any kind are expressed or implied. Readers acknowledge that the author is not engaging in the rendering of legal, financial, medical or professional advice. The content of this book has been derived from various sources. Please consult a licensed professional before attempting any techniques outlined in this book.

By reading this document, the reader agrees that under no circumstances are is the author responsible for any losses, direct or indirect, which are incurred as a result of the use of information contained within this document, including, but not limited to, —errors, omissions, or inaccuracies.

Table of Contents

Introduction

Chapter 1: Getting Started to Decluttering Your Mind

Chapter 2: Shifting Your Mindset: From Cluttered Negative Thinking to Clutter-Free Mental Clarity

Chapter 3: Why your Mind is Filled with Clutter - And How to Fix It

Chapter 4: Effective Meditation - Being in the Present Moment

Chapter 5: Organizing Life Priorities: What Matters the Most

Chapter 6: Managing Daily Tasks for Better Productivity and to Avoid Getting Overwhelmed

Chapter 7: How to Achieve Work-Life Balance

Chapter 8: Remaining in the Moment at Work

Chapter 9: Home Management 101: How to Effectively Declutter Your Home

Chapter 10: Choosing a 'Less is More' Lifestyle for Worry-Free and Stress-Free Living

Chapter 11: Taking it to the Next Level with a Tiny House

Bonus Chapter: Getting Rid of Digital Clutter to Maximize Technology Use and Simplifying Your Life

Conclusion

DECLUTTER YOUR MIND	PEACE	FOCUS
	BALANCE	CLARITY

Introduction

Congratulations on owning *Declutter Your Mind* and thank you for doing so. Making the decision to clear out your mental clutter once and for all can be a difficult one and for that, so give yourself some credit.

Unfortunately, there is often far more to it than that as mental clutter is an often insidious threat that can be difficult to pin down, even if you are looking for it. To help you reach your goal successfully, the following chapters will discuss everything you need to know about clearing your mind of excess clutter as quickly and easily as possible.

Inside you will learn everything you need to know about mental clutter, how it forms and what you can do to get rid of it. You will find a variety of tasks and exercises designed to do just that, as well as a few designed to help you take things a bit farther still by doing things like decluttering your physical space and considering minimalism in all its forms. You will even find a bonus chapter that discusses the perils of digital clutter and what you can do to stop it from forming once and for all.

There are plenty of books on this subject on the market, thanks again for choosing this one! Every effort was made to ensure it is full of as much useful information as possible, please enjoy!

Chapter 1: Getting Started to Decluttering Your Mind

Chapter 1: Getting Started to Decluttering Your Mind

1.1 Understanding Mental Clutter

It is easy to see the way clutter builds up in the real world, slowly but surely it can take over a shelf, a room, maybe even a whole home. Mental clutter is much the same, sticking in the corners of the mind and slowly building until it is difficult to get a single thought in edgewise that isn't part of the existing paths your mind has built to deal with the detritus.

In order to move forward with the process of decluttering your mind, you are going to need to clean out all of your mental clutter and start fresh. What's more, dealing with mental clutter isn't something you will only have to do once after you have cleaned your mental house, you are going to need to learn to remain ever vigilant to ensure that it doesn't start building once more.

Mental clutter is the stuff that keeps us stuck in self-sabotage, suffering, struggle, stress, and separation. It is the stuff that makes life hard and complicated. It is the stuff that puts us at odds with everyone else.

Hidden where eyes can't see, mental clutter lurks wherever peace and love don't. As long as we're cluttered, we're resisting the flow and ease of life.

If you are not experiencing clarity, peace, and love, you have mental clutter. It lives exclusively and elusively in your thoughts. It starts as a head-fog, cloudy and misleading, and evolves into something much bigger.

Clutter composes the stories we tell about ourselves that cripple our potential and attack our well-being. It says we can't, we shouldn't and we won't. It gives cause for doubt and mistrust, leaving us feeling helpless in the world.

1.2 Benefits of removing mental clutter

Removing the mental clutter that is blocking up your mind is essentially like removing individual layers from an onion. In this scenario, if you want to get at the truth of the way the world looks around you, and you haven't cleaned out your mental clutter in a while, then that truth is covered in various layers of misinformation, beliefs (accurate and inaccurate) related thoughts and stories you tell yourself. Luckily, as long as you take the time to clear out your mind from time to time, the effects of mental clutter aren't permanent.

If you have ever spent a prolonged period of time feeling more deeply connected to the universe and the people around you, then the good news is that you can feel that same sense of unity, love, and peace at all times, that was a moment when all of your mental clutter was cleared and you were free to operate at maximum efficiency.

Unfortunately, most people are far more focused on the state of their bodies than they are their minds. This focus on eating right and staying fit is compounded by the desire to work as much as possible, which in turn can make it difficult to find the time to exercise and eat right. This issue is then compounded by the needs of others that they want to help meet, their own needs that need to be met in order to keep the whole process moving and a million other little things fight for their time.

This frequently means the mind gets the short end of the stick, but this can be far more detrimental than you might expect. The fact of the matter is that every other aspect of your life, from relationships to your career, to your body all hinge on the health of your mind. Thus, if you don't find the time to nurture your mind and clear out the mental clutter then everything else is sure to suffer sooner or later.

When it comes to decluttering your mind, the ultimate goal is always going to be clarity and a sense of peace that can't be manufactured in any other way. You will feel a return to a state of almost innocence where you are free from any drama, dogma or stigma that you might be holding onto. While you might feel as though these are the things that prop you up at first, with time you will see all they are really doing is holding you down.

1.3 Looking for symptoms of mental clutter

One of the most nefarious parts of mental clutter is the fact that many of its aspects serve to mask the fact that there is an issue in the first place. As such, if you have let your mental clutter build up unchecked for years, then you may be extremely cluttered without even realizing it. If you are worried this is the case, consider the following list of symptoms and see if they apply to you.

1. *Confusion:* Do you find yourself frequently confused by things that you used to handle with ease? A sense of general confusion, often accompanied by either fear, worry, or both; as well as a general sense of feeling scatterbrained are all signs you may be dealing with an influx of mental clutter.

2. *Chatty inner voice:* Everyone has a mental narrator who operates in the back of their mind to some degree. If that voice seems to never shut up, then you may be dealing with an influx of mental clutter. If your inner dialogue goes from normal amounts to what amounts to a constant noise in the background, then this should be considered a red flag of potential mental clutter.

3. *Chaos:* While there are always going to be certain events in our lives that sow disorganization, and chaos when they appear, this should be the

exception, not the rule. As such, if you find that you are always dealing with a large amount of chaos in your life, either physical or mental, then you may need to take a closer look at your mental clutter and see if that isn't part, or all, of the problem.

4. *Conditions:* When it comes to mental clutter, having an influx of conditions can also be thought of as having lots of requirements, stipulations or prerequisites on your daily routine or the activities and events you take part in most frequently. If lately, you have been feeling as though everywhere you turn there are limits, rules, and boundaries, either external or internal, then you may be dealing with an influx of mental clutter.

5. *Collections:* If you are someone who has always been drawn to the idea of having the complete set of something, then taking an analytical approach to your desire to collect may be difficult. Unfortunately, this can be a clear sign of increasing mental clutter which means it is important to find a way to measure your collections that makes sense for you. If left unchecked, mental clutter can increase one's desire to stockpile physical representations of past success as a means of increasing feelings of security and comfort. After all, the cluttered mind reasons, if I'm feeling extra anxious keeping these things around will make me feel better. A good indicator that your desire to collect has gotten stronger is if you have recently begun to expand an existing collection or if you have just started an entirely new collection.

6. *Comparisons:* If you generally tend to classify yourself as a happy person, but recently find yourself looking at those around you and feeling as though the things you have don't really stand up, then mental clutter could well be to blame. This sort of desire is often generated as a result of an unfulfilled desire to seek out better and more interesting activities or challenges, often those that are just over the next hill. If you find yourself

comparing yourself to those around you more regularly than before, mental clutter may well be to blame.

7. *Worry:* This is one of the most potentially dangerous types of mental clutter of them all. What makes worry so insidious is that it can make not just the time before a specific event occurs unbearable, it can also limit your full potential and make any negative outcome you were stressing out about much more likely to actually come true. Worry will also make it far easier for you to look at the world in absolutes as opposed to more realistic shades of gray.

8. *Guilt:* Guilt is a difficult type of mental clutter to excise as once you have given into it you can easily become trapped in a scenario where your worst mistakes are played back to you endless while you are left wondering what you could have done differently. If not handled properly this can lead you to a cycle where the only real outcome is despair and it becomes increasingly difficult to even consider trying anything new. While guilt in certain situations is perfectly understandable, if not exactly healthy, you will be able to tell if your guilt is the result of mental clutter if you find yourself retaining deep feelings of guilt for relatively minor issues.

9. *Negative self-talk:* Self-criticism can be beneficial if restricted to a healthy measure. However, there is a limit to the amount of negative conditioning you can subject your mind to before it starts becoming counter-productive. There is a sea of difference between, "I really need to be more physically active" and "I am a lazy blob." Excessive self-loathing can heavily backfire because it shifts the focus from ways through which we can improve to our failures. Over a longer period, thrash negative self-speak can up your stress level, and lead to major depression. Learning to tame negative self-talk is the key to overcoming challenges, feeling more confident and achieving the life of your dreams.

10. Negative self-talk is another type of mental clutter than can be difficult to pinpoint, especially if it has been building for quite some time. The key, then, is to keep a list of the types of things you find yourself saying to yourself throughout the day. While these negative quips might fly under the radar at the moment when you look back on them after the fact the pattern should be far more pronounced.

Long-term effects: If left untreated in the long-term, mental clutter can potentially throw you completely out of sync with your thoughts, leading to a feeling as though there is an overall lack of harmony in the world at large. In fact, the feeling of mental fog that you feel can ultimately evolve into a crippling form of malaise that has the potential to last for weeks, months or even years. In so doing it has the potential to cripple your potential in all aspect of your life, making it difficult to believe or trust anyone, even those closest to you. You will also lose faith in your abilities and find it difficult to deal with the world at large. This is why it is vital that if you find any mental clutter you do what you need to do in order to eradicate it posthaste.

Your Quick Start Action Step: Create a baseline
The first step towards finding mental clutter is to take stock of the current state of your mind. This can be something that you write down, or it can be something you track mentally, what matters is that you take a flashlight to all the various corners and little used rooms in your mind and take stock of what you find there. Look in all the places you would expect to find mental clutter and see what you find.

Not only will doing so provide you with a roadmap of things that you will need to focus on in the near future, but it will also provide you with a baseline that you can measure yourself against in the future. This way you will be able to track how much progress you have made, sort of like a before and after photo that some people take while working out. Regardless of your preferred method of analysis, you should keep some concrete record so that you have something to look back on during moments of self-doubt or when it seems as though you aren't making progress so you can see how far it is you have really come.

Chapter 2:
Shifting Your Mindset: From Cluttered Negative Thinking to Clutter-Free Mental Clarity

Chapter 2: Shifting Your Mindset: From Cluttered Negative Thinking to Clutter-Free Mental Clarity

2.1 Fixed and Growth Mindset

As children, some people are told they excel in certain subjects while others are told that they succeeded because they tried hard and that effort leads to success. The first group of children can be expected to develop a fixed mindset whereby their brains become more active when they are being told how well they have done. The second group of children can be said to have a growth mindset wherein their minds are the most active when they are learning what they could do better next time. Those with a fixed mindset tend to worry more about how they are seen by others than what they are actually learning which is why those with a growth mindset tend to be more successful in the long run.

Fixed Mindset
- Wants to look smart or competent regardless of the reality
- Quick to avoid challenges
- Easily thwarted by obstacles
- Thinks effort is "pointless"
- Ignores feedback
- Can feel threatened by the success of others

Growth Mindset
- More interested in long-term results.
- Enjoys a challenge.
- Learns from obstacles
- Equates effort with success
- Appreciates criticism
- Finds inspiration in the success of others

The two mindsets also manifest themselves differently when it comes to dealing with setbacks. When those who have a fixed mindset are met with a setback it directly affects how they see themselves because it shakes their belief in their innate talent. This makes it easier for them to give up on something they are struggling with as they can easily tell themselves that it is just not a talent that is in their wheelhouse. On the other hand, when a person with a growth mindset is met with a challenge they instead worry about the best way to overcome it and treat the issue as an opportunity to learn and grow.

By this point, it shouldn't be hard to see which of the two mindsets is going to be more prone to acquiring mental clutter, and also which is likely required in order to clean out your mind once and for all. A fixed mindset is particularly dangerous in this scenario as it can balk at the work ahead in hopes of finding an easy workaround. This is something that you simply can't abide, however, and if you hope to clear your mind you are going to need to make a conscious decision to focus on this situation with a growth mindset and never look back.

2.2 Change for the better

With the consequences of having a fixed mindset so potentially disastrous, especially if you are striving to find the inner strength to clean out your mental clutter once and for all, it is important to do what you can to break these negative mental habits as quickly as possible. Luckily the human brain has the ability to constantly reshape itself throughout the course of its lifetime which means that it is never too late to shift into a growth mindset, no matter how deeply rooted the fixed mindset principles might be. New neural pathways in the brain can be formed as new thoughts are repeated time and again, and once they become well-worn paths, then new habits are formed.

When it comes to creating new neural pathways, one of the best ways to do so is by seeing a noticeable result from an action that you consciously took in an effort to change your mindset, such as the exercises described below that will help you experience a mind that is clutter-free. While a single positive choice or two a day won't generate noticeable results on their own, their cumulative effect can be substantial and that typing point can occur sooner than you might think.

While you are getting used to keeping up a growth mindset on the regular, you may find that remaining positive and feeling empowered is easy as long as everything is going well, only to have things fall apart as soon as the struggle is added to the equation. Those who originally had a fixed mindset are going to have a much more difficult time powering through times of adversity at first, but if they ever hope to find a way to truly empower themselves then they will need to remain positive and see it through as that is the only way that new neural pathways are ever going to be successfully formed.

When working to keep a growth mindset in all things, it is important to keep it up even when the going gets tough. It will likely seem like the easiest thing in the world to do while things are going well, but a fixed mindset is much more likely to manifest itself during times when roadblocks begin presenting themselves. Your fixed mindset will likely make you want to abandon all hope of forward progress when these road blocks appear.

In this case, it is important to make an effort to stop thinking of the challenges as roadblocks and start thinking of them as opportunities for you to learn and grow. Finding personal ways to meet the challenges that come your way head on without dwelling on them unnecessarily is the first step towards making a real change for the better. If you are having difficulty putting this idea into practice, consider the following:

- Take the time to look for the silver lining and consider what opportunities that meeting this challenge head on will give you access to. Dealing with problems as soon as they arise will typically provide you with the opportunity to handle the issue in a simpler fashion or take actions to stop the situation from otherwise getting out of hand. Learning to appreciate this opportunity will make adopting a growth mindset much easier.

- Use the challenge in question as a mirror to reflect challenges you might be having when looking to improve other facets of your life. If everything is going smoothly then it can be easy to overlook important information that could come back to bite you later if left untreated for too long. Dealing with challenges directly can, in turn, then provide you with insight into what else in your life deserves a closer examination.

- Consider the possible reasons behind why you feel the way you do. When you are face to face with roadblocks you will often find that they are easier to approach if you have a growth mindset as it will allow you to take that extra moment to stop and really consider whatever it is that you are going through. A quick run through of the facts will often reveal the fact that roadblocks will be easier to overcome than they might have at first. This is often thanks to a personal bias that you were harboring that you likely didn't even know was affecting you. If your deeper analysis reveals that the road block is more mental than physical, you need to be comfortable in your growth mindset to let the mental block go.

2.3 Experience a Clutter-Free Mindset

The exercises in this section have all been chosen to help you start to get used to the type of clear, clutter-free mindset you should be fostering. You won't need to worry about forcing a clear mindset in these scenarios, all you need to do is focus on the task in question and the desired mindset should manifest itself. Once you get used to this new and improved mindset, you will then be ready to start actively working towards it more regularly.

1. *Brain writing:* Take a piece of paper and, as quickly as you can, write down any issues that come to mind. Keep writing until you have nothing

more to add. Next, take a look at your list and acknowledge that you will deal with these concerns at an appropriate time.

With this out of the way, you will find that you are now free to devote yourself fully to the task that you originally wanted to focus on. Ideally, you will want to take a journal and fill at least three pages each morning. Hand written is important in this case, not in digital form. The kinesthetic aspect of writing in longhand form is a key to its effectiveness.

The content of your morning pages can be anything that's on your mind. Even if the thoughts you're writing are negative, putting them on paper is cathartic for the mind; this simple technique helps to clear out your mental cobwebs so you can devote yourself more fully to the creative tasks each day holds. It's like taking a dust-buster and poking it around into the corners of your mind. By transmuting these thoughts into physical form, on paper, you can set them aside – both literally and figuratively – and enter your day more refreshed and creative.

The same technique works equally well in group brainstorming sessions. Plan for some "warm up" time to get participants into a creative frame of mind, just as you would stretch prior to exercising. Solicit the group's top of mind thoughts and ideas but – here's the important part – don't stop there. The first ideas that brainstorming participants throw out are typically the obvious solutions, and they tend to be of fairly low value. Keep pushing the group farther outside of their comfort zone via a variety of playful activities and ideation exercises. This is where some of the greatest insights and highest-value ideas will likely emerge.

2. *Play Music:* Playing music is a popular creative outlet. While any type of music is equally effective, if you aren't serious or talented with an instrument, it should serve you even better as a mental decluttering

exercise because you have no objective to improve. Your only goal is to play.

If you already play an instrument, you know what to do: just spend some time with it and zone everything else out. Make this a session in clearing your mind, rather than in getting good at a song or writing something new that others would enjoy. In other words, don't try to perfect your Canon in D, but rather play something you already know and don't have to think about, or just mess around with simple scales and progressions.

If you don't already play an instrument, pick up one of these instruments that require little to no knowledge to begin messing around:

- Hand drum or Djembe
- Gong
- Singing Bowl
- Chime
- Kalimba
- Maracas
- Your voice (There's a reason why singing in the shower is so fun — it feels good.)

A popular instrument that requires zero talent is the Kalimba, an African instrument typically made out of a coconut shell and 5-8 metal keys. It becomes meditative and there is no way you can make a mistake. Ukuleles are also fun instruments to pick up even if you have no experience with music. They only have four strings, and the strings tend to be softer since they're nylon, and so easier on your fingers. Learn a couple of strumming patterns and a few chords and you'll be well on your way to enjoying the mini string instrument.

Remember, the purpose isn't to wow an audience — it's to focus your attention on creating rhythm, melody, and sound.

3. *Go for a Hike:* Nature and exercise are both prescriptions for improved health and well-being. Henry David Thoreau made a good point when he said, "I took a walk in the woods and came out taller than the trees." It's because nature feels good. It nourishes the body, mind, and spirit. Combine them and what you get is time well spent. Countless poems have been written and studies have been published about the benefits of nature and the sheer awe and magic that it can offer.

    Find a hike near you. Try searching AllTrails.com to find a new route. As you hike, bring awareness to your breath as you move. Notice the sensations in your body, observe how your heart rate increases on the hills, and watch your calves engage as you descend. Notice every detail of your surroundings, the colors, the plants and fauna, any animals you pass, the rhythm and pace of your movements, and your feet as they hit the ground in a cyclical manner. Take it all in without distraction.

4. *Watch a Sunset:* A great way to instill yourself with a present feeling is by watching the sun say goodbye for the day. Aside from its natural beauty, the sunset is also a brilliant reminder that each and every day offers us a new end and a new beginning. Get lost in the vibrant colors and spirit of the sunset and take Mother Nature's advice that the rest of your to-do list can wait until morning.

5. *Work in the Garden:* While it would be easy to blast music while you plant your petunias, try to cultivate a quiet, mindful state of being as you work in the garden. If you can keep the music off and your mind focused on paying attention to what you're doing in the garden — the sensations of your hands in the dirt, the breeze across your face, the smell of the incoming

basil, and your breath as you move, you can turn your gardening session into a mindfulness practice.

6. *Dance:* Put on some trance or ambient music without words, close your eyes, and allow your body to move freely. Try using an open space like the yard, living room, or basement, and dance like no one's watching because, well, no one's watching. And it feels good.

7. *Bake:* Baking requires focus. You have to follow the directions precisely, otherwise, you could end up with a hard, burnt, inedible object when your family is eagerly awaiting banana bread. Choose a recipe that you've never tried before and one you may consider complicated, make sure your ingredients are out on the kitchen table, (and make sure you have them ALL, otherwise your exercise in mindful baking could quickly turn frazzled,) and begin.

    As you follow the steps, pay attention to your breath and the task at-hand. When you mix the batter, turn the spoon or whisk slowly and mindfully, taking in the smells and changes in texture along the way. As you spread the batter into the pan, take extra care in making sure it's even and smooth. When your treat is ready, follow the steps at the end of this post to eat mindfully, enjoying every morsel of your masterpiece.

8. *Write a Note:* Choose someone in your life you appreciate and write them a handwritten note. Perhaps it's to thank them for something they did, the type of person they are, or maybe it's for no reason at all except to tell them the things you admire about them.

    Before you begin writing, close your eyes and picture an image of this person in the center of your mind. Take a few breaths. Notice what feelings come up when you have this person at the center of your mind.

Now jot down a list of 5-10 things about this person — adjectives that highlight their talents, words that describe how they make you feel or how they've helped you, or anything else that would make them feel good.

Now write them a note using your list as fuel. If you want to get extra fancy, you can include a small gift of gratitude and hand deliver it. Otherwise, you can send it in the mail. Cultivating awareness and gratitude can be helpful tools in supporting your mindfulness practice. Plus, it will doubtlessly make the day of this special person in your life.

Your Quick Start Action Step: Pay Closer Attention
With the proliferation of screens across all forms of technology, people are increasingly being rewarded for dividing their time among as many different tasks as possible. As a result, there is far less time to focus on the smaller details of a given situation and consider the types of meaning that are only found upon closer consideration. Therefore, the first step in becoming more perceptive is going to be taking note, not of what you are missing, but of the fact that you are missing it.

To get started down this path, all you need to do is stop for a few moments once or twice a day to consider what is going on around you and think about how much you are currently missing out on throughout the day. The specifics here don't matter, as long as you slow down and take the time to look at life from another angle. This could include something adventurous like hiking a new trail every weekend, or it could be something simple like making a point of noticing what your coworkers are wearing each day, the specifics don't matter as long as you work on it each day and start building a new skill in the process.

Chapter 3:
Why your Mind is Filled with Clutter - And How to Fix It

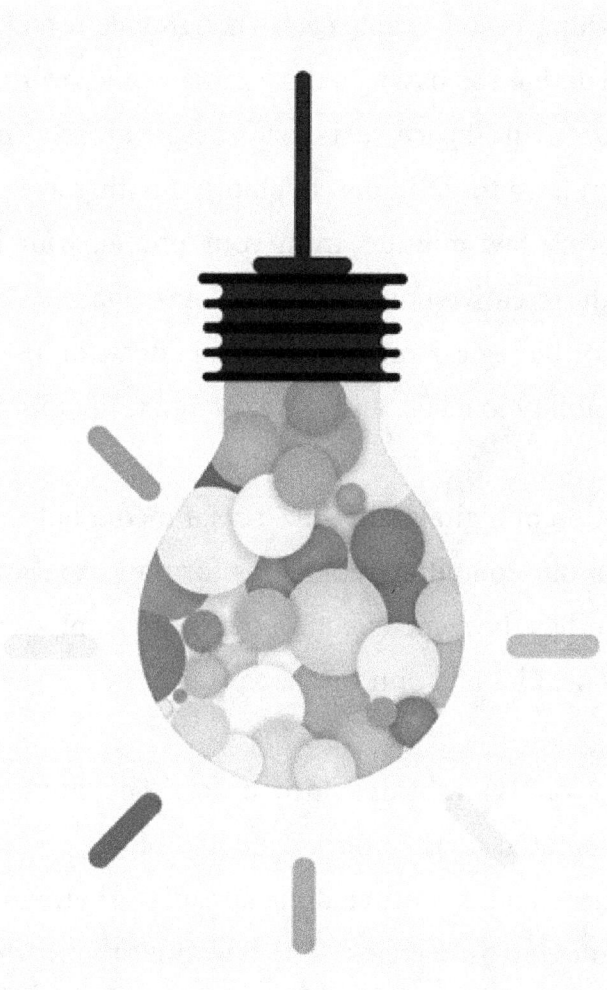

Chapter 3: Why your Mind is Filled with Clutter - And How to Fix It

3.1 Your brain on clutter

Described as anything that is kept, even though not used, needed or wanted, clutter can also be defined as having a disorganized and overwhelming amount of possessions in our living space, cars or storage areas. But clutter isn't just physical. When you have to-do items constantly floating around in your head, or you hear a ring every few minutes from your phone, your brain doesn't get a chance to fully enter creative flow or process experiences. Clutter creates stress that has three major biological and neurological effects on us—our cortisol levels, our creativity and ability to focus, and our experience of pain.

The overconsumption of digital stuff—like social media notifications, news feeds, games and files on our computer—competes for our attention, creating a digital form of clutter that has the same effect on our brain as physical clutter. Neatness and order support health—and oppose chaos.

So, what is going on? Our brains love order. The human body consists of thousands of integrated and interdependent biological and neurochemical systems, all organized and operating along circadian rhythms, without which our bodies would disintegrate into chaos. It's no wonder that the organization within our very own bodies naturally extends to the desire for order and tidiness in our homes. And order feels good, in part, because it's easier for our brains to deal with and not have to work so hard.

3.2 The science of cortisol

No matter the ways, reasons, and means by which the creep of stuff exceeds our ability to mentally and physically manage it—all of it amounts to stress. Clutter can trigger the release of the stress hormone cortisol, which can increase tension and anxiety and lead to unhealthy habits. Cortisol is a hormone produced in response to stress by the hypothalamus-pituitary-adrenal axis (HPA).

Chronic clutter can create prolonged stress, throwing us into a state of low-grade, perpetual fight-or-flight—the system designed to help us survive. The fight-or-flight response involves the complex interaction of many body systems and organs that activate needed functions and minimize unnecessary functions during times of stress. These systems must remain in balance to maintain optimum physical and psychological health.

According to a Cornell University study from 2016, stress triggered by clutter may also trigger coping and avoidance strategies, like eating junk food, oversleeping or binge-watching Netflix.

If we are not stressed, we get most of our cortisol in the morning to get us going. Levels taper off the rest of the day if we are relaxed, enabling us to enjoy psychological and physical wellbeing. But a messy home environment can prevent our body's cortisol levels from naturally declining throughout the day. Taxing this system eventually results in higher levels of depression and anxiety, and a lower capacity to think clearly, make decisions, and stay focused.

To supply the body with the energy needed to deal with stress, there are several physiological changes that occur with elevated cortisol levels:
- Diversion of blood flow to the muscles from other parts of the body
- Increased blood pressure
- Increased heart rate
- Increased blood sugars
- Increased fats in in the blood

If there is no relief from stress, all of these changes are bad for healthy brain activity and can cause lasting negative changes in brain function and structure. Additionally, when stress raises the body's cortisol levels, its overall health can be adversely affected, including organ damage, the suppression of the immune, endocrine and reproductive systems, the lowering of the metabolism, and the disruption of the sleep cycle, to name a few.

It is difficult to maintain a state of wellness over time when the body's energy is channeled into coping with stress.

Just as concerning, when the body is in a state of chronic stress and not thinking clearly, the brain tends to only see that which is negative as these are, historically, the things that could turn into threats. Unfortunately, all this does is reinforce the pre-existing sour point of view, perceived lack of social support and subsequent poor interrelationships.

Research from a 2009 study out of UCLA's Center on Everyday Lives of Families (CELF) has shown that women who perceive their homes to be cluttered tend to have unhealthy patterns of cortisol levels. A team of professional archaeologists, anthropologists, and other social scientists studied the home life of 32 middle-class, dual-income families with 2-3 children of ages 7-12 in Los Angeles. In the study, family members recorded self-directed home tours describing objects and spaces in their homes, during which saliva samples were taken at regular intervals to measure cortisol levels.

The data were collected for three days and compared to and correlated with vast amounts of other data previously collected over the course of four years. According to the CEFL study, the amount of stress women experience at home is directly proportional to the amount of stuff they and their family had accumulated.

It's interesting to note in the UCLA study that men did not exhibit the same results, having normal cortisol fluctuations. Presumably, they were not as stressed by the amount of stuff in their home. This can be explained possibly by the results of other studies that have shown that the home is traditionally perceived as women's domain and ultimate responsibility, even in households where both partners work.

Other studies also support the finding that if men don't think the responsibility of keeping the house tidy is relevant to them, they may not be inclined to see the clutter and so are not as stressed about it.

This may be explained further in part by research that has indicated that there are distinct differences in vision between men and women since men have 25 percent more neurons in their visual cortex, a part of the cerebral cortex that processes visual information. The irony is that even though the visual cortex of a man has more neurons than a woman's, men are impacted more by the things they see that they think have to do with them, and less by the things they think do not.

The brain has a limited capacity to process information. To filter out extra stimuli and focus on what we are trying to achieve at any given moment, the top-down and bottom-up attention mechanisms compete. By mutually suppressing each other, brain power is exhausted, and ultimately we lose focus. Whether we know it or not, a kitchen counter stacked with mail and basket full of unfolded laundry can be as distracting to us as a toddler in the throes of a tantrum.

3.3 Start to declutter

Now that we know what all of our extra stuff is doing to our health and ability to function, it's time to get rid of it, right?... Oh, but if it were only that easy. Although most people don't experience heightened ACC/Insula activity to this degree, we can all identify with the feeling of angst when finally tossing that pile of unread magazines, or those ticket stubs from last summer's trip to New York to see Hamilton. The good news is, those who suffer from hoarding respond well to Cognitive Behavioral Therapy. For the rest of us... there is decluttering.

In addition to improving your mood and focus, decluttering often acts as a catalyst for taking better care of other aspects of our life. By purging unneeded items from our homes, it is like deleting files to create disk space on your computer. Suddenly, the whole operating system is more efficient…this decreases stress and increases your effectiveness personally and professionally.

While actually going ahead and getting rid of unnecessary items will be covered in detail in a later chapter, the exercises in this chapter are going to cover the preparation you will need to do in order to get ready to declutter once and for all. This lifestyle change requires two things: a vision list, and a why list. You will want to start with your vision list. This list is going to be everything you want to accomplish from your future results. Your list can, and should, contain anything that is important to you and serves as a reason for why you are making this lifestyle change. The more unique and personal this list is, the better it will serve you.

If you are having a hard time getting started, here are some things you might consider writing on your vision list:
- I want to eat healthier at every single meal
- I want to experience the loving relationships in my life, every day
- I want to contribute to the world in a meaningful way, daily
- I want to read and write on a daily basis
- I want to be passionate about every single day that I'm alive
- I want to take risks in life
- I want to be present in every single moment

These visions are essentially what you want to accomplish through your minimalist lifestyle. After you are clear on what you want to achieve with your new lifestyle, you want to get clear on why. Understanding why you want change is what will compel you to actually make the change. So, after you completely your list that outlines everything you want, you can start a list right beneath it that is going to tell you every reason why you want it. You should make sure that both lists are as detailed as possible. If you have several important items on your vision list, and on your why list, that is completely okay. You should not feel as though you have to limit yourself. The more reasons you can provide, the easier the entire transition is going to be for you.

As you become more aware of what you want, as well as why you want it you should find that it becomes easier and easier to motivate yourself to actually start working towards achieving your dreams. While you may feel as though your good intentions are strong enough to get you through right now, not listening to your mental clutter can be more difficult at the moment than you might expect. That is why it is important to have your vision and your why. These are lists you will refer back to when you are feeling internal resistances. You can regroup, refocus, and start all over again in a new frame of mind that will allow you to have an easier ability to achieve your desired results.

Your Quick Start Action Step: Start working on your vision list

As discussed above, your vision list is the linchpin that holds your motivation together. You don't need to put it together all at once, however, if you need some time to work on it that is perfectly fine. You can keep a running tally of things to add to it whenever you think of a new one. This process doesn't have to stop either, you can add something new to your vision list whenever the need strikes you.

Chapter 4:
Effective Meditation - Being in the Present Moment

Chapter 4: Effective Meditation - Being in the Present Moment

4.1 An ancient practice

Mindfulness meditation is a type of meditation which focuses on being as aware of each moment as possible, thereby helping the consciousness to expand by forming a stronger connection with the present. Mindfulness meditation has a long history of practice as part of the Buddhist faith where it is revered for its ability to improve both mental happiness and physical well-being. This has been corroborated by research which shows that mindfulness meditation is a beneficial treatment for a variety of mental conditions. What's more, it has also been shown to be effective when treating conditions including anxiety, stress and drug addiction.

While mindfulness can be practiced almost anywhere at nearly any time, the concept began as a structured meditation technique practiced by Buddhists known as vipassana. Roughly translated this means to live in the moment while understanding that sometimes you must be aware of the future as well. The general idea is that achieving vipassana will allow you to come to understand the universe as a whole and comes through the knowing of a few key principals.

The idea of practicing mindfulness first caught on in the Western world in the early part of the 1970s. Professor Jon Kabat-Zinn is credited with creating a mindfulness based method of stress reduction which paired mindfulness with yoga to great result. While Zinn didn't do anything particularly new, the fact that his techniques led to measurable improvements for a wide variety of ailments both mental and physical in turn led to additional studies on the topic. These studies have shown time and again how effective practicing mindfulness can be which in turn has led to a steady increase in the practice to the point where it can now be found being regularly practiced in schools, veteran treatment facilities, hospitals, even prisons.

4.2 Many benefits

In addition to helping improve self-discipline, studies show that that taking 15 minutes out of your day to practice mindfulness meditation has a host of additional benefits as well. For starters, it is known to show dramatic increases when it comes to projecting a strong sense of self while at the same time noticeably reducing stress. This is thanks to the positive effects that mindfulness meditation has on attention span, emotional regulation and body awareness. What's even more impressive, neuroimaging has shown that mindfulness meditation actually allows those who practice it to process information more quickly than those who do not.

The activity can also literally improve the health of the brain as studies show that those who started practicing mindfulness meditation at a young age actually have more volume in their brains as they age. Meditating regularly is also known to increase the thickness of the hippocampus which means that it actually makes it easier to learn new information and retain it for a prolonged period of time. It also positively affects the amygdala which means those who meditate are less likely to experience stress, anxiety, and fear. With so much going on under the hood, is it any wonder that those who meditate tend to report an overall increase in mood, temperament, and wellbeing?

Beyond these noticeable physical changes, regularly practicing mindfulness is known to help improve self-discipline in additional ways by decreasing instances of meditators' minds getting stuck in negative thought patterns while also making it easier to focus for prolonged periods of time. A recent Johns Hopkins University study found that practicing mindfulness meditation regularly is equally effective at treating anxiety, depression, and ADHD as many commonly prescribed drugs.

Other reasons to practice mindfulness meditation

- Mindfulness meditation naturally leads to a deeper understanding of the self and allows many people to take stock of their strengths and weaknesses, leading to personal growth.
- Studies show that those who practice mindfulness regularly have a stronger memory, leading to an easier retention of facts in both the long and the short term.

- In addition to the specifics, mindfulness meditation improves overall physical wellbeing with those who practice regularly reporting fewer instances of illness and a more rapid recovery when they do fall ill.

- Mindfulness meditation can help improve emotional control while at the same time increasing one's threshold for pain.

- As surprising as it might seem, making a habit of being mindful can actually make even the most middling music seem more engaging. This deeper level of engagement leads to a general increase of enjoyment, regardless of the type of music or any previous musical preferences.

- With a regular dose of mindfulness meditation, many people experience a dramatic increase in their ability to empathize with others no matter what the situation. Furthermore, it allows practitioners to listen to other viewpoints more actively, more compassionately and results in their ability to withhold judgement on thoughts and ideas that differ from their own.

4.3
While practicing mindfulness meditation might seem like a tall order at first, the truth of the matter is that being mindful is a habit which means you can learn to improve through practice, practice, practice. In fact, it should be one of the easier habits in this book to get accustomed to as it is as easy as taking a few moments

out of your day to focus exclusively on the present via all of the information that your senses are bringing in.

1. *Getting started:* When you first start practicing mindfulness, it is important to always practice at the same day to ensure your body is going to get into the habit of entering a mindful state each and every day, to make the transition easier to manage. Don't forget, it takes about a month for a new habit to solidify in your mind which means that as long as you can keep it up for that amount of time you can keep it up indefinitely.

   In order to reach a state of mindfulness, you are going to want to find someplace comfortable, and quiet to sit, though not so quiet and comfortable that you are tempted to fall asleep. Then, all you need to do is breathe deeply, in and out. As you breathe in, focus all of your attention on the information that your senses are providing to you, focus on the way the air feels in your lungs, how it smells and how it tastes. Slowly but surely, expand your consciousness so that you are taking in as much information about your surroundings as possible.

2. *Observe the moment:* Mindfulness is not necessarily quieting the mind or finding an eternal state of calmness. The goal here is simple. We want to pay attention to the moment we are in without judging. When we judge a thought or something we may have done in the past, we tend to dwell on it. That isn't living in the moment and is not conducive to mindful meditation. While this is easier said than done, it is a crucial step to mindful meditation. With practice, it will be easy to achieve. Be mindful of the moment, of your senses and your surroundings.

3. *Ignore those pesky judgments:* Take notice of the times you are passing judgment while practicing. Make note of them and move on.

4. *Always come back to observation and the present moment:* It is easy for our minds to get lost in thought. Mindfulness meditation is the art of bringing yourself back to the moment, over and over, as many times as it takes. Don't get discouraged. In the beginning, you will find your mind wanders a lot. Reel it back in and keep moving forward.

5. *Be kind to yourself:* Even if your mind does happen to wander, and it will, don't be hard on yourself. It happens. Acknowledge whatever thoughts pop up, put them to the side and get back on track.

Practice mindfulness at all times
Once you get the hang of the basics of mindfulness meditation you will find that there is practically nothing you can't do that doesn't lend itself to being mindful. The following are some of the easiest ways to get into the habit of practicing mindfulness meditation around your home, but you can also practice at work, on public transportation, or even while driving. With a little extra practice, the wide variety of times you can easily slip into a mindful state are sure to surprise you.

Interact with social media mindfully: While it may seem surprising if you go about doing so in the right way, spending time with Facebook or Instagram can actually be a very mindful experience. While it is easy to get distracted from your goal while interacting with social media, with practice you will find that the time you spend doing so can leave you feeling quite centered and ready to face the next challenge that awaits you.

In order for this type of mindfulness to be effective, the first thing you are going to want to do is to limit potential distractions as much as you can. This is crucial due to the fact that most people interact with social media while multitasking which will make practicing mindfulness much more difficult. Once you have cleared the distractions out of the way you will then want to clear your mind and focus on the moment as much as possible. After you have found the correct mindset, you will then want to revisit old pictures from activities you were a part of and try your hardest to relive those events as thoroughly as possible.

With each picture you see, do your best to try and remember everything you were doing at the moment. Think back to the way you felt and really let the experience wash over you. Throw yourself back into the moment with all your might and remember the various signals your mind was bombarding you with at the time. After you have returned to the memory, take the time to think about how the space that you are once again occupying smelled, as well as the physical sensations. Remember the way the temperature felt on your skin, the sounds of the memory and the things your ears were focused on whether you were actively aware of them or not. With enough practice, you will realize that you have the ability to block out virtually all of the stimuli in the present day and exist solely in your memories.

Your Quick Start Action Step: Start the day off right

It doesn't matter what drink you use to start off your day, be it coffee, tea or something else, you can use that time to practice mindfulness which can, in turn, start any day off on the right foot. If you do it properly you can use the sensations, you experience with your morning cup to pull you into the moment with more clarity than most other activities. This may be the only peaceful moment you are going to get in the entire day, make it count.

1. Start the morning with your first mindfulness session in mind. Focus on the thoughts you have as you begin to wake up and take note of them without expressly interacting with them. Continue this mindset for as long as possible, stopping before you begin to make your morning beverage.
2. While making the drink, focus on the anticipation of the act, consider the feel of your hands as you prepare the beverage and the other sensations that the act of creation provides.

3. Find a good spot to sit quietly for a moment and focus of the drink. Consider the way the cup feels in your hands, the smell of the drink and the way it looks.
4. Now slowly take your fist sip, consider the taste of the drink, the way the liquid feels as it moves across your tongue and down towards your stomach.
5. As you drink consider how the beverage makes you feel, consider what benefits it is providing your body to ensure you are able to meet the challenges of the day head on.
6. Pay special focus to only these thoughts as you consume your beverage. If you find your mind wandering, gently bring it back to the task at hand.
7. After you are done, take an extra moment to hold the cup in your hands and be as present at the moment as possible.

Chapter 5:
Organizing Life Priorities:
What Matters the Most

Chapter 5: Organizing Life Priorities: What Matters the Most

5.1 Deciding what is important

Everyone has had that sinking feeling where they realize that they have too much on their plate but are unable to do anything about it. After all, if every task feels as though it is equally important, how do you know where to begin. While it can be easy to feel overwhelmed if you find yourself in this situation, it is important to understand that it is one that everyone has found themselves in at one time or another and, more importantly, it is certainly not impossible to juggle a variety of seemingly competing responsibilities or priorities, it only feels that way at the moment.

The biggest issue in these instances is determining what is actually important and what only feels that way. After all, even if everything feels equally important at the moment you will still need to determine where to start. The most effective means of doing so is through the use of the triple constraint which is a triangle with each side representing one aspect of the task you are contemplating. One side represents the costs of the task, one represents the scope of the task and one represents the time required to complete the task and none can be adjusted without affecting the other two.

As an example, if you were planning to pain your guest bedroom before you have guests next month, then you wouldn't be able to change the scope of the task which is to paint the room, but you could adjust how much time you want the job to take and how much the task might cost because you could hire painters to do the task for you.

5.2 Be proactive

While it can be easy to want to plan out your priorities when you feel as though you are getting in over your head, it is far more productive to do so on a regular basis precisely so you can keep yourself from feeling unduly overwhelmed. After all, if you feel as though the walls are already closing in then you are going to have limited options when it comes to improving your situation. If you take the time to deal with the issue when the high-pressure period is still a ways off then you are more likely to come up with an easy solution to avoid it all together. Regardless of when you decide to go ahead and establish your priorities, it is important to stick with the habit and never look back regardless if you are using them at work, at home, or throughout your everyday life. After you really understand the things you need to work on, as well as how long they take, you will be able to make smarter decisions when it comes to whether or not you can take on a new task in the first place.

5.3 Check your priorities

In order to ensure that your priorities are currently where they need to be you are going to want to evaluate them individually using the following process.

Make a list: The first step in this process is going to be thinking back through the past three months with the goal of making a list of everything you want to improve, everything you want to change completely and everything you want to work to maintain as is. When looking at your life you are going to want to break your list down into categories, or pillars, that all support your primary goal at the moment. Common pillars include work, health and fitness, personal relationships, finance, and personal life though your pillars should reflect your personal situation.

This initial list is not going to represent your list of goals per se, this list is more freeform than that, instead what you are working on here is the list of core needs that your goals will strive to solve. For example, one of your cores could be to lower your stress level. You could then come up with a goal that would help you to do so in a reliable way. Using your cores as guidelines for the goals you set will allow you to ensure that your goals have a purpose which will, in turn, make it easier to ensure you see them through.

Organize your list: Once you have a general idea of some goals, you will want to ensure that your list of things that you want to improve, change and maintain is being represented in full across your pillars. If there are any extra goals not being covered, consider putting them on the backburner for the moment until you free up some more mental space. After all, there is only so much you can realistically deal with at one time. If you try and do too much at once you run the risk of not actually succeeding at anything.

Add more specifics: Once you have a general idea of your goals and the pillars that they work to support, the next step is to make them as specific as possible which starts by considering which can be completed most easily as well those that will generate the greatest overall benefit in return for the work that you will be putting in. If you are working towards a goal that you are confident you will succeed in then you will want to start with those that will generate the most benefit in the long-term. However, if you are working on a goal that is somewhat out of your wheelhouse you will want to start with the easiest goal as this will help build your confidence and make it easier for you to tackle more complicated tasks.

Judge your goals as a whole: Once you have a general outline for the goals you plan on tackling in the relatively near future, the next step is going to be looking at them as a whole and deciding if they reflect not only who you want to be but also who you are. Put another way, it is important to ensure they hit on all your pillars in a way that can be completed without moving heaven and earth.

Choose where to begin: While it can be easy to get caught up in the planning stage, especially if you are dealing with multiple goals at once, it is important to not use the planning as an excuse to never actually get started. Eventually, you need to be confident in the plans you have made and actually put the rubber to the road. After all, your priorities will never be fulfilled if you don't actively start working towards your goals.

Your Quick Start Action Step: Make your goals SMART goals

SMART goals are specific: Good goals are specific which means you should be able to concisely express them in just a few sentences. They should provide you with a clear idea of the requirements for reaching your goals along with any constraints that may prevent you from reaching them successfully.

SMART goals are measurable: When the goals you choose are measurable it will be clear to you how you will be able to tell if your goal has either been a resounding success or an absolute failure.

SMART goals are attainable: A good goal is one that is realistically attainable which means that you understand any potential roadblocks that may stand between you and the goal in question and that they will be ultimately surmountable.

SMART goals are realistic: A good goal is one that is realistic in addition to being attainable which means that you can expect success without something extremely unlikely being required to push reality into your favor.

SMART goals are timely: A good goal is one that as a clear timetable for when it is going to be completed. Even the best-intentioned goals are likely to fall apart if their timetable is to strict, but also if it is too generous.

Chapter 6: Managing Daily Tasks for Better Productivity and to Avoid Getting Overwhelmed

Chapter 6: Managing Daily Tasks for Better Productivity and to Avoid Getting Overwhelmed

6.1 Discipline is key

While those who are currently in the midst of a bout of depression, lethargy, angst, or whatever other state their mental clutter has left them in, might find it hard to believe, those who are empowered are prone to feeling these things as well. The biggest difference then is that those who are empowered have the self-discipline to not let those feelings get in the way of whatever it is they need to do. While teaching your mind to have a growth mindset is a great first step, improving your self-discipline will make it easier to be more productive and to avoid feeling overwhelmed regardless of how much mental clutter you are currently dealing with.

Being as productive as possible means taking the time to completely understand the intricacies of whatever the task you are currently undertaking turns out to be. The simple fact of the matter is that if you are aware of all of the potential issues the given task might face, you will be able to deal with them much more appropriately when they do manifest themselves. When it comes to empowerment, this means that you are going to want to dig deep on yourself and determine what is truly holding you back so that you can to work on correcting the source of the issues hampering your empowerment, not just its symptoms.

Being truly self-disciplined means knowing when it is best to wait and gather strength and resources and when it is best to strike for optimal efficacy. It doesn't matter how much fact-finding you have done if you never go ahead and pull the trigger. Having self-discipline means acting to work on the issues that are hampering your quest for empowerment, even if they are difficult to face directly. Having self-discipline is a skill which means that the only way it is every going to get easier is with practice. You need to have the dedication to your overall improvement to power through, with the understanding that making the s self-disciplined choice will get easier each time you choose to make it.

6.2 Be ready for what's next

Those who are truly self-disciplined, are that way because they have put in the time required training themselves rigorously to do so. The commitment they have shown isn't something that just appeared overnight, it was the sum of months if not years of dedication to the idea of self-improvement based around the idea that self-discipline is a trait worth fighting to achieve.

On the other hand, at the end of the day, those who have shown commitment and dedication to bettering themselves in the name of self-discipline, get to know the deep, pure satisfaction of being proud of their hard work. The road ahead may be long but the results will certainly be worth it. If you preserve you will be able to stand among the greats and know that you are truly ready for whatever life choses to throw at you next and that you have the self-discipline required to succeed at any and every task yet to fall before you.

When you start actively working to improve your overall level of self-discipline, be aware that it will be one of the most difficult challenges you have ever faced. If you have never actively cultivated self-discipline before then your mind will be trained to prioritize instant gratification which means that it will be set to fight you tooth and nail for what it perceives as your own good. Your own mind will be your greatest enemy but if you persevere you can reach the ultimate goal at the end of the rainbow.

Eventually, however, with enough hard work you will develop the confidence in yourself that is required in order to practice self-discipline all of the time, whenever it may be required. If you master your own mind, there is nothing you can't accomplish keep this in mind and use that perseverance to achieve your goals.

6.3 Check your schedule

1. *Make a schedule:* When it comes to making a schedule, the first thing you will need to do is find the type of calendar or planner that is right for you. It can be a physical item or an application on your phone, the specifics of it don't matter as long as they work for you in such a way that you are sure to use them consistently. Whatever you choose, it is important to keep all of your scheduling to a single application or day planner as opposed to splitting activities into their own calendars, the goal is to integrate fully, not segregate information and make it more difficult to access and remember.

2. *Analyze your schedule:* With your entire month spread out in front of you, this is a good time to take a long hard look at how you truly spend your time. Use this as an opportunity to trim the fat as needed, but also to expand on areas that you feel are important but are currently neglected. This is the point where you can most easily make changes that you feel the need to, don't be afraid to put thought into action, the only one that can improve the ways you spend your time is you.

When it comes to prioritizing tasks, it really is as simple as making a list with pros and cons for each of the potential uses for the time in question. You can't be everywhere at once, no matter how hard you try; what's more, no one expects you to be. Be self-confident enough to let others know when you have no more time for additional commitments and you will feel a lot better in the long run. This is the point where you have to make decisions about your time, don't put them off any longer.

During times when you have a large number of tasks to complete in a very specific amount of time, you can then use a similar set of criteria to determine the most effective order to complete them in. When considering the most efficient means of doing so it is vital that you take into account several factors beforehand. For starters, if a specific task looks to be quite tedious but is still more or less straightforward, you will still want to get it out of the way first as it will give you a mental boost and make anything that comes next seem less cumbersome by comparison. However, if one task is significantly more difficult than the rest you may want to set it aside for later so that you can give it your undivided attention when you do decide to tackle it.

3. *Allot timeframes:* Once you know the right order for the tasks you are going to complete, you will want to spend some time thinking about how much time in your schedule you want to devote to each. While scheduling all of your tasks directly back to back might seem like a natural choice at first, it is likely to come back to haunt you as soon as one activity takes slightly longer than normal and all of your other tasks end up behind as a result. Scheduling can be your enemy but it can also be your ally if you let it. As a general rule of thumb, you are going to want to plan out the time you need for each activity, plus travel time, plus 10 minutes because you never know when something isn't going to go according to plan. After all, the worst that can happen is that you end up 10 minutes early for your next meeting.

Your Quick Start Action Step: Clear your schedule of distractions

If you always feel as though you are running just a little bit late, then it may be because you have too many distractions competing for your time. Before you go ahead and plan out your schedule as described above, make sure to remove any unnecessary distractions first to ensure you aren't budgeting time to account for them without realizing it. The first thing you will want to do is to take a look at your day to day schedule and see what, if any, distractions are common amongst more than one activity. If this ends up being a person or activity that you end up spending lots of scheduled, but also unscheduled, time with then you might need to make dramatic changes, at least until you develop new and improved habits.

Assuming this person or thing takes up a good portion of your time without producing much if any, obvious benefit then there are a few questions you will want to ask yourself. First, consider if the distraction provides you with a means of blowing off steam and relaxing which is not otherwise included in your schedule. If this is the case then what you see as a distraction is actually performing a vital function by providing you with some relief that the rest of your schedule is lacking. If this is not the case then you will instead need to consider if that time might be better used in another way.

Chapter 7:
How to Achieve Work-Life Balance

Chapter 7: How to Achieve Work-Life Balance

7.1 Finding a balance

With technology connecting employers to employees (and freelance workers) after working hours, it's become increasingly tough for people to establish a legitimately healthy work-life balance. You certainly have the right not to tackle work during your personal time, but the fear of losing your job or contracts can add pressure to making yourself available around the clock.

According to a Harvard Business School survey, 94 percent of workers admit to working more than 50 hours a week, and nearly half worked 65-hour weeks. The stress from increased hours and staying plugged into work after hours not only affects your health but can also damage your relationships and overall happiness.

By following a few simple guidelines, it's possible to start shifting the weight toward greater work-life balance.

7.2 Why you need to pull your plug

The technological revolution has made it increasingly easier for people to connect with each other around the world, which has opened the doors for more telecommuting positions within companies. However, just because you can be online all the time does not mean you should be, especially for home-based workers who don't have as obvious a separation in their work-life balance.

Stanford business professors found that workplace stress adds $125 to $190 billion per year to America's health costs. Overworking alone accounts for $48 billion of that total. Ironically, the brunt of health care costs are then covered by the employers who have often established systems that are the source of the stress. In this situation, not only do the employers suffer financially, but there are also other negative consequences on the business due to the decreased productivity of overstressed employees.

Because these costs often seem hidden, they are not properly factored into employers' cost-benefit analysis.

Within the European Union, the costs of overstressed employees are being taken seriously. Some large European companies have now taken steps toward reducing burnout and creating a better work-life balance.

In 2012, Volkswagen blocked emails to employees after-hours, while Daimler moved to delete emails of employees on vacation. After the email was deleted, the sender would receive an email similar to I am on holiday. I cannot read your email. Your email is being deleted. Please contact Markus or Linda if it's an urgent matter or re-send the email after I return to the office on November 12.

Both Germany and France have also made moves to rein in employers. In 2014, Germany banned managers from calling or emailing staff after work. More recently, France enacted a law that bans after-work emails.

However, if you are telecommuting and working across time zones, it can be hard to unplug, especially if there are no laws protecting your work-life balance. Nonetheless, it's as important, or perhaps more important, for you to do so.

7.3 Set the right boundaries

Beyond being healthy, unplugging gives you clarity and perspective. Unplugging also gives you the space you need to let other thoughts and ideas surface. When you are always on, you don't allow other things to the surface that might be more important.

1. *Notice distractions:* Stop the distractions, get your projects in line. Additionally, it makes you feel more in control of yourself and your life, which has a huge impact on overall happiness. When you find it difficult to unplug, conduct a quick self-assessment:

   - Is it force of habit?
   - Is it because you frequently check social media?
   - Is it to deal with FOMO about the latest scoop?
   - Is it a form of procrastination?
   - Is it because you are frequently behind schedule and forced to put in more hours?

   By establishing the reasons you struggle to unplug, you can start to better understand what mental attitude you need to adopt to make time to be offline.

   If you're unwilling to unplug for what might be considered workaholic reasons, determine if your work schedule is overloaded or if you are making systematic mistakes that are impacting your efficiency.

   Are regular distractions, such as social media or co-workers, interrupting your workflow? Probably. The average worker enjoys no more than three minutes of work without distractions. After an interruption, it takes 25 minutes to refocus, which is detrimental to your efficiency. By establishing what work and life goals you want to prioritize, it's possible to eliminate distractions. To do this, create a list of the top three tasks you want to accomplish for the day, week, and month. If you get those three things done, that day, week or month will be considered productive. Anything you accomplish beyond those is simply a bonus.

2. *Learn to prioritize:* Prioritization also involves knowing what you want out of life, such as physical health or time for your family. Once you've

identified what's at the top of your list, you can make adjustments to your life and schedule to make sure they don't end up on a back burner. By knowing your priorities, it is easier to say "no" to distractions that will drain your energy and resources away from what is most important to you.

If you tend to say yes without thinking when you're asked to do something extra, stall. Don't answer straight away. Say you'll get back to the person asking, then use that time to think clearly about whether to say yes or no. If you want to say yes, fine. But if you want to say no, say no and keep saying it. Don't justify your actions or give excuses. There's no need to be nasty or rude.

Saying "no", doesn't mean you have to turn down work. If a task that is going to ruin your workflow and have a negative impact on your priorities for the day pops up out of the blue, tell your coworker or client that you can do the project, but not until tomorrow (or whenever is best for your timeline).

3. *Work Smarter, Not Harder:* The old adage work smarter, not harder, is more applicable now than ever as distractions through social media and demands on your time continue to exponentially increase. The key to working smarter is strictly managing your time. Do not fall into the trap of multitasking. Multitasking is a work-place myth used to justify constant distractions: both internal and external. The mind can focus on only a little information at any single moment, which means that any attempt to multitask will lead to scatter-brained results. So, focus solely on the task at hand, whether it is putting the final touches on a presentation or tossing around a baseball with your son.

Imposing a strict schedule for your work will provide structure for focus. People often get distracted by emails, so establish set times for checking email, replying only to the ones that merit the time of your response.

4. *The Pomodoro technique:* The Pomodoro technique can also help you create structure in your schedule. It sets aside 25 minutes of your undivided attention for the task at hand. Then, you rest for five minutes. As you become more adept at using the technique, you can slowly increase the time. However, if you reach the point that distractions start slipping in, scale it back.

   Given that you can do a full-body workout in as few as seven minutes, it should be no surprise how much work you can accomplish during a focused, 25-minute session. Be just as strict with yourself during your rest time; rest is an important part of the system, as it allows your brain to relax and recover.

5. *Leave on time every day:* The most important step to managing your work schedule, and creating the ideal work-life balance, is to leave work when your working hours are finished. Even if you telecommute, by establishing a clear work space and hours, you can give yourself the same release from work as anybody sitting in an office. Knowing that you won't start checking work emails at 10 p.m. that night helps keep you focused during working hours. By following these general rules, as well as other productivity techniques, it is possible to work smarter, not harder.

6. *Let go of Perfection:* Many people think that procrastination is caused by a person's laziness, disorganization or apathy, but it couldn't be further from the truth.

   Usually, procrastination is caused by one of four reasons:

   - Low energy level
   - Lack of focus

- Fear of failure or success
- Perfectionism

By this point, you should have some ideas on how to improve your focus, and as you establish a better work-life balance, you'll improve your energy levels. That said, these last two reasons for procrastination can be the downfall of smart, dedicated workers. It can be very hard to let go of perfectionism, especially when it's been ingrained in you as a child. Many overachievers found it easy to balance everything when they were younger, but struggle as they enter the adult world and are looking to find the ideal work-life balance.

Perfectionists face three major issues at work: overworking, failing to delegate, and fear of failure. All of these problems can lead to a snowballing effect of projects piling up on your already full plate.

It's easy to say "let go of perfection", but how do you actually do it?

First, realize that perfectionism is no excuse. If you tell your boss, colleagues, or clients that the delay is because "you want everything to be perfect", you aren't getting any sympathy. Late is late. Second, focus on progress, not perfection. Some perfectionists clam up at the start of a project because they can see the big picture, but don't know how to break it down into smaller steps. It's important to start doing something that moves you toward the end goal, no matter how small that step is.

Lastly, show self-compassion. Forgive yourself and acknowledge that mistakes are part of life. The law of diminishing returns establishes that at a certain point there will still be mistakes, but the energy and time it takes to rectify them no longer outweighs the benefits.

7. *Make Time for Yourself:* You work hard. Give yourself credit for that and treat yourself well. By incorporating enjoyable forms of exercise into your daily schedule, you will not only be healthier, but you will also have more energy to tackle your work. Say goodbye to overtime and nights at the office.

By working these two practices into a daily routine, they will both become second nature. There will be an adjustment period. However, once you find the rhythm, you'll discover that you enjoy both more and more each day. Beyond regular breaks in the office, such as those prescribed in the Pomodoro technique, take a vacation. While on holiday, allow yourself to shut off your phone and close your laptop so that you can relax and unwind. By letting go while you're on holiday, you're more likely to return to work invigorated and focused.

Finally, don't forget that there is more to your life than sleeping and working. Set aside time in your schedule to take up a hobby. Even the busiest, most successful people pursue hobbies, as they enrich their lives and help bring depth and meaning to what they do.

Your Quick Start Action Step: Track your time

In order to ensure that you can eventually get your work/life balance to the right place, the first thing you are going to need to do is to track how much you are currently working so that you can see where you need to improve. While tracking the amount of time you spend working each week it is important to do so for at least a month and then average out the hours. You should also pick a month that represents the full variety of your tasks if possible. During this time it is also important to ensure that you work as you would normally without doing anything out of the ordinary that would affect your results. After all, if you skew the results then the only person you are going to be hurting is yourself.

If you work a salaried position, then this should be a relatively easy step as it becomes about not letting your employer take undue advantage of you. If you are an hourly or freelance employee, however, then this step will also require that you sit down and put together a budget based on the amount of work you currently do as well as the amount of work you would be doing if you adjusted your work/life balance accordingly. While it can be tempting to work as much as possible, especially if you are a freelancer and the work isn't always available, making a change may be easier if you look at it as making taking a hit in the short-term in exchange for a prolonged amount of work you can do effectively in the long-term as you won't have to worry about mental clutter.

Chapter 8: Remaining in the Moment at Work

Chapter 8: Remaining in the Moment at Work

8.1 The Sad Truth

For many people, the work day is a time for lots of stress, with little left over when it comes to mitigating it properly. Mindfulness is a great choice for use during the work day not just for the ways it helps decrease the symptoms of depression, anxiety, and stress but also for the ways it can help you focus on the task at hand. In addition, the boost to empathy will make you more liked around the office in addition to being more efficient.

Practicing mindfulness at work can help you turn your reactions into reasoned responses. A reaction is a nearly automatic action which takes place in response to a set of stimuli while a response comes to a stimulus after a thorough assessment of the situation. If you spend enough time in the moment, then a moment starts to feel like more than enough time to come to a reasonable solution.

Practicing mindfulness can also train you to come at new problems in a different way. First, it is important to instead think of the problems as challenges to be met. A challenge is something that can be bested and learned from, two things that being mindful prepares you for quite readily. Consider writing down the challenge and spending a few moments focusing on it and its solutions, odds are you will then find it much easier to come up with a solution.

8.2 A Net Positive

While not possible with all professions, with practice you will find that you can squeeze in a few minutes of mindfulness meditation here and there throughout the day. While the individual efficacy of any particular mindfulness meditation session might be relatively minimal, the overall gestalt will lead to a sense of wellbeing that is greater than the sum of its overall parts. While it might seem difficult to deal with the demands of the day, the demands of your coworkers and everything else that life throws at you, you can consider each micro mindfulness meditation session as islands of calm in an otherwise choppy sea. Mindfulness in the workplace should be thought of as a tool that allows you to squeeze every bit of efficiency out of the workday as long as you think carefully about how to use it as effectively as possible.

While it might seem that making an effort to practice mindfulness in the office will lead to an overall decrease in productivity, the reality is that the opposite is true. Especially if you have a particularly hectic job you likely find that you often have to react to things without thinking through all the possible outcomes of your response. With your head cleared from frequent micro-meditations, however, you will find that the moments in which you have to make important decisions naturally seem to expand in order to provide you with all the time you need to make the right choice, right now.

Remember, when you react to something you at taking a nearly automatic action, letting the stimuli that sent you down this path take control of the situation. However, if you respond instead of react, then you are making a well-reasoned choice based on all available data. Reasoned responses lead to better solutions every single time.

8.3 Getting Started

Mindfulness in the workplace should be used as a tool for the purpose of squeezing out every last bit of efficiency from the day that you can, by ensuring you think as carefully about how to use it productively as possible. If you are already using your commute to practice mindfulness, then when you arrive at work you will already be in a mindful state that will allow you to get the most out of each moment. In order to keep the mindfulness train rolling, you will want to take a moment or two between tasks in order to focus on your breathing and thus the sensory data that your body is providing.

This doesn't need to be the sort of elaborate process that you learned to complete at home, it should only take a minute or two to ensure your head remains on straight throughout the day. Quantity trumps quality in this situation and if you practice each time you switch tasks you will find that your early-morning mindfulness state persists throughout the day. This is not to say that you fail if you can't take a moment to be mindful between every set of tasks, as long as you fit it in when and where you can, you will come out streets ahead in the long-term.

For many people, clearing their mind during the work day can be extremely difficult. If your job leaves you little time to sneak in a bit of mindfulness, then simply start with whatever you can get, even if it is just 30 seconds. Over time, you will get a feel for when you can sneak in 30 seconds of solace and learn the best way to chain dozens, if not hundreds together throughout the day.

Clearing your mind in the middle of the work day can be tricky, but like with all type of mindfulness, each time you do so will make the next time that much easier. Don't push yourself unreasonably, however, starting with just a few micro mediations each day is still a great effort in the right direction. If you work in an office, any time you need a moment to catch your breath, and you want that moment to last as long as possible, consider the following. Otherwise, alter it for your situation as needed.

1. As you breathe in and out normally, be aware of the breath in your lungs before expanding that awareness outward.
2. Become aware of your fingers as they glide across the keyboard in front of you, listen to the sound of the keys pressing as you go about your business. Focus on the decision to press each key and the resulting actions that come into play because of it.
3. Focus on your body, straightening your posture to its ideal limits and taking in the sensations being given off by the lower half of your body.
4. Take one more breath and let the rest of the world back in to continue on about your day as normal.

Additionally, any time you find yourself in a meeting or a particularly long conversation with a coworker you can use the opportunity to slip into a mindful mindset by simply focusing on what the other person is saying to the exclusion of everything else that is going on around you. Remember, being mindful isn't about being choosy when it comes to which moments you are fully present in, it is about embracing the now in all its many forms.

If you spend a large portion of your day either responding to smartphone notification or emails, then you can find some time to practice mindfulness by simply taking 30 seconds between each reply to center yourself and briefly be mindful. While 30 seconds might not seem like much, you will be surprised at how powerful the cumulative effect can be. Think about it this way, if you respond to 100 email or notifications in a day then you are really giving yourself nearly an hour each day in which to be mindful. Once you give it a try, you will likely find it hard to give up.

If your job requires that you sit in one place for most of the day then it is also important to double check on your posture before you get started. You can do this by relaxing all of your muscles, starting with your neck and extending the exercise all the way down to your toes. You will then want to reverse things and go the other way, starting at the bottom and working your way back up to your neck. After you are relaxed you should find that you are more easily able to handle the signals that your body is sending out, making it easier for you to determine if you have any pain points you have been ignoring that you can easily deal with.

If your job fins you repeating the same more or less mindless task throughout the day then you can use this opportunity to practice mindfulness. Any activity that includes a physical activity as well as the need to focus on one thing in what is more or less a passive way is a great way to set yourself up for a mindful experience. All you need to do is to put all of your focus on the task at hand and you should be able to spend your day in a mindful state.

In order to maximize the effectiveness of your end of day commute and the mindfulness meditation you are hopeful going to practice during that time, you should take the last five minutes of the work day to put aside everything that has happened, both good and bad, while you were on the clock. During this time you will want to think about all of the things you have been able to accomplish, as well as those things which you had to put off until tomorrow and even the things you just plain missed the boat on. You will then want to consider all of this in light of the bigger picture and thing about what it all means long-term. Finally, with the day truly done you will then want to close the door on it and leave any unsolved problems alone until tomorrow. Remind yourself that tomorrow is another day and let yourself move on with your day free from your work day cares.

Quick action step
The best way to ensure that you can continue to be mindful throughout the work day is to take steps to help yourself develop a mindful mindset before you even get to the office. A great way to do so is by commuting mindfully.

Start as soon as you get into your vehicle by vocalizing your intention to be mindful during your morning commute. Then take a few deep breaths and use this time to become more aware of your body. Become aware of your hands on the steering wheel and what they feel beneath them. Become aware of your body and the sensations it feels as it is pressed against your seat. Feel your foot on the pedal and the resistance it feels as you prepare to drive. As you begin your drive take in the world around you while at the same time striving to be aware of the act of seeing, of the act of hearing. Try to focus on these three things, body, sights, sounds and only these things for the length of your drive.

That's really all there is to it, though like many things it is much easier said than done. Today's society is obsessed with multi-tasking and as such your mind will want to wander, thoughts will try and sneak their way in, you will want to think about the things waiting for you at work or tasks you left unfinished at home. Your phone will make at least one noise and you will be tempted to see the specifics of the notification. It is important to ignore these obstacles. Likewise, it is important to not dwell on these thoughts or distractions that are given into as that is, in reality, another thought trying to sneak its way in. Instead, you must acknowledge the errant thought or temptation and let it go without interacting with it further. Over time you will find that the process of existing at the moment will become easier while also noticing a wide variety of additional benefits as well.

Chapter 9: Home Management 101: How to Effectively Declutter Your Home

Chapter 9: Home Management 101: How to Effectively Declutter Your Home

9.1 **Face the facts**

Not many of us are natural minimalists. Plenty of us are more, let's say, maximalists. Clutter seems to be magnetically attracted to us and honestly, we're secretly waiting for a knock on the door from the producers of the show *Hoarders*. That's why it can be quite a relief sometimes when it comes time to move someplace new. Finally, you're forced to go through all of your possessions with a fine tooth comb, and you have the chance to really clean up your act by giving your whole household a thorough decluttering service.

Keeping only the things you love or that are useful and getting rid of things you no longer need or want, helps you create a life that is more streamlined. And it allows you to live in a home where you can find things more easily and where you'll spend less time constantly tidying up piles of accumulated belongings.

The bonus of giving your household a decluttering service right before you move is that you will have fewer items to pack and transport, and so the whole moving process will be faster, easier and cheaper. Even if this is not the case, however, you will still find that decluttering your home is worth the effort.

9.2 **Less can be more**

A study by Pamela Thacher, assistant professor of psychology at St. Lawrence University in Canton, N.Y., found that people who sleep in cluttered rooms... are more likely to have sleeping problems. This includes having trouble falling asleep at night and experiencing rest disturbances. Additionally, people who make their beds every morning experience longer, more restful sleep, especially when they use fresh, clean sheets.

Researchers at the University of Minnesota found that people who spent time in an unorganized room were twice as likely to eat a chocolate bar than an apple. And researchers at Florida State University reveal a link between hoarding and obesity, noting that people with extremely cluttered homes are 77% more likely to be overweight.

If you start to minimalize your possessions, you open your home up to all kinds of potential that you may not have seen while the home was cluttered. You will be able to find everything that you need with minimal effort, allowing you to devote more time to living life to the fullest. You will also understand that filling the home up with junk isn't productive or valuable because it takes away that freedom and not only that – it costs money.

Imagine being able to access a cupboard or closet and find what you want straight away. Imagine being able to leave a room as clean as it was when you entered it. It sounds clinical and cold to some people but in fact, they may be kidding themselves into a false sense of security because the truth is these spaces don't have to be cold. They can, in fact, be welcoming because they encourage the mind to work with more than the stuff that is in the home. This stuff has become a talking point between people but when you take it away, true conversation flows that is meaningful.

Express yourself: You get a chance to express your own creativity instead of having it imposed upon you by all of your possessions and you begin to remember what life is all about and change your values. Your focus will not be on keeping the house clean and tidy. It will do that almost on its own. That means your focus can be used on creativity, enjoyment, and leisure. That gives you more time, more money, less stress, and a more abundant lifestyle! See how less can be more?

You'll spend less money: When a major goal of your style of living is to have less stuff, it's almost guaranteed that you're going to end up spending less money on goods, products or services. With the internet at our fingertips, it can sometimes be difficult to curb our spending. Along these same lines, another common mode of thought is the idea that if you make more money, then all of your financial problems will go away. When you chase more and more money, your consumption often becomes more and more problematic. One day you'll look around and think that you have it all; a large house, a fancy car, and lots of stuff that fits inside of your lovely consumption-driven life. What you'll most likely be missing is substance and a sense of joy. Don't allow these ideals to dominate your lifestyle. Spend less, own little tangible goods, and lead the happiest life that you can. It's that simple.

Reduce your stress: Stress can cause physical ailments in the sense that it contributes to premature aging, those pesky grey hairs on your head, and even memory loss. What's more, clutter in the home is known to shift our attention away from what we are truly trying to focus on. We have enough stressors in our life; we don't need our stuff to provide with more reasons to worry.

If you want to test your own reaction to how you react to clutter in your home, you can try this small experiment. Find one messy countertop in your home (this may be easier for some people than others). Next, take the time to really clean off another countertop in your home. After you've done this, look at each countertop separately and gauge your internal reaction to each one. It's probably not surprising that you are most likely going to find that the clean countertop is going to provide you with a sense of calm, while the messy countertop is going to shoot some kind of stress indicator into your brain and body.

9.3 Keep, sell, throw

1. *Overview:* There are many ways to successfully purge. Some decluttering experts advocate the Four Box Method, where the idea is to go through each room in your home, armed with separate boxes: one for things you

want to keep, one for items to sell or give to charity, one for things to chuck, and one box for things you're still undecided about.

Others are devotees of the Japanese KonMari method, where you pick up each item you own and decide to keep it only if it "sparks joy" or if it is useful. There's even "Swedish death cleaning", a new decluttering technique where you downsize your belongings in recognition of the stark fact that one day, you won't be able to take anything with you, and that your junk will only be a burden for your loved ones. But hey, if that's too much for you, you might prefer to stick with the Four Box Method.

Whatever method you use, most decluttering experts advise tackling only one room at a time, rather than attempting to declutter your whole house in one go. Give yourself enough time to ensure you don't stress out and become overwhelmed with the magnitude of the job. But if you're moving soon, and want to get it all done asap, don't be afraid to call in help from a professional decluttering service, which can be surprisingly affordable. Experts advise tackling only one room at a time, rather than attempting to declutter your whole house in one go.

2. *Get a friend to help:* As shows like *Hoarders* have demonstrated, the problem is usually with our psychological attachment to objects, rather than there being any physical difficulty in picking up items and placing them in boxes or garbage bags. Sometimes, what you really need is a truly objective person to help you with the task of discerning trash from treasure. That's where hiring someone who offers a decluttering service can make things so much easier.

Don't mistake the idea of a decluttering service as involving a stranger coming in and charging about, dumping your prized possessions in rubbish bags with reckless abandon. It can be as harmless as having an assistant follow you around, taking your directions, but also being critical enough to say.

Or you may go the whole hog and engage someone to assist you with a full decluttering service by completely reorganizing all your belongings, room by room: sorting and tidying and removing excess clutter–with your approval naturally.

Your helper can undertake all kinds of decluttering tasks, like organizing your DVD and CD libraries, or rearranging your kitchen cupboards and pantry or reorganizing your clothes. They can also be tasked with making repeated trips to dispose of junk. And in the end, once you are sitting in a beautiful, tidy, organized home, you'll find packing up for your move and unpacking in your new house an absolute breeze.

We're all familiar with the mantra 'a place for everything and everything in its place', even if that place is concealed beneath a million other absolutely essential objects. In recent years, a whole industry has built up to encourage us to rid ourselves of possessions that clog up our lives or, at least, our hallways.

3. *Objects must 'spark joy:* 'Spark joy' is the phrase that launched 1,000 skips. It comes from *The Life-Changing Magic of Tidying Up*, written by Japanese decluttering guru Marie Kondo, which has sold more than five million copies. One of the reasons that attempts to declutter stutter, stall and then fail is that books and websites assume we can breezily ditch a lifetime of memories and possessions between walking the dog and breakfast. They don't adequately acknowledge that, if you live in a house filled with cherished inherited and acquired objects, it's incredibly daunting. It's easy to ditch an Ikea chest of drawers, yet not so easy to get rid of the ormolu cabinet you inherited but hate.

4. *Decide if you are a collector or a discarder:* Your brain is hardwired to be a collector or a discarder. Here lies the first stumbling block. Grandpa's desk is much harder to send off to the auction house than any old desk. Just as you should never name a pig you intend to eat, if you are to surround ourselves only with the things we love, we need to stop giving our possessions names. Try to think of it as the desk or, better yet, simply a desk.

It's not really about the thing, is it? For example, if you have a hideous cut-glass bowl that belonged to your grandmother and it's the shape of a grape, quite the most unpleasant thing, but you'll never get rid of it. To throw it away would be like throwing away the memory of her. That doesn't seem right, does it?

5. *Own your own space:* Throwing away things that are tied in with your memories of people absolutely fine it's really important to own your own space and not have other people's stuff invading it. Things have memories vested in them, but if they're not actually giving you pleasure, then let them go. When it comes to tackling those important family pieces that inspire more guilt than love, your first step should be to offer it to other members of the family. You look generous and it mitigates guilt. And it's telling if nobody else wants it, isn't it?'

Ultimately, a soothing, peaceful, happy-to-get-up-in house is what it's all about. Keep your eye on that prize and get cracking. You have nothing to lose but (someone else's) junk.

Your Quick Start Action Step: Take it slow

- Start small, with a drawer, a cupboard or a heap of photographs. Each small success is incredibly motivating.

- Banish thoughts of perfectionism. It's crippling and holds you back. Do what you can. Keep going.

- Declutter first, shop second. Tempting as it is to dash out and buy boxes, cartons and crates, it's displacement activity for the gritty business of throwing things out.

- Don't wait until you can get everyone in your house on board. If necessary, allow the permanently messy a limited area in which to express themselves. Fly-tying kit in the study – yes. All over the kitchen table – no.

- You can get rid of wedding presents and still remain married in the eyes of the law.

Chapter 10:
Choosing a 'Less is More' Lifestyle for Worry-Free and Stress-Free Living

Chapter 10: Choosing a 'Less is More' Lifestyle for Worry-Free and Stress-Free Living

10.1 Take the plunge

Minimalism is one of those concepts, like "eating healthy" or "being a good person" that has a somewhat different meaning depending on who you ask. This is perfectly natural, as adhering to a minimalist lifestyle is a personal choice that means something different to everyone who makes it. Again, while your personal mileage might vary when it comes to this definition, many people believe that minimalism is the focused elevation of the things that matter most in life, coupled with the discarding of everything that prevents you from focusing on those things on the first list. More simply put, it is about understanding what is most important to you and acting on that knowledge to the best of your ability.

Living your life in an intentional way is a core part of living a minimalist lifestyle which includes considering the values in life you feel matter the most and then doing everything you can to align your life in such a way that these values take up your time as well as your space. This is precisely why minimalism will look different to everyone because if you ask 100 different people what they would prioritize most, you would get 100 different answers.

There are two different ways to look at this lack of specificity. On one hand, it can be difficult to know if you are starting off on the right foot because the first step is going to be different for everyone. On the other hand, however, it means you can create the unique minimalism framework that is right for you.

Minimalism was a style that actually started coming into popularity in the 1950s. The intention of minimalism is not to do your best to live without anything you want or need. Instead, it is an opportunity to free yourself from material possessions. Through living the minimalist lifestyle, you can attain freedom from: fear, worry, overwhelm, guilt, depression, feeling trapped, and more. As a minimalist, you are not required to throw away nearly all of your belongings and live in a constant state of lack. Instead, it is about learning not to give your material items more value than what they're actually worth in life.

10.2 **Free yourself**

As you adhere to the minimalist lifestyle, you will start to notice long-term effects settle in. These symptoms are pretty much always positive.

People who live the minimalist lifestyle for a while generally note that they feel burden-free. They don't feel a constant responsibility to look after an obscene number of items that they cannot care for, either due to lack of time or lack of desire to. They do not feel guilty for letting things they "should" like sit unused and unappreciated. They do not feel depressed when they look around and see stuff everywhere that is being unused, or not cared for. Instead, they feel completely burden-free! They do not need to spend any more time worrying about, accounting for, or looking after stuff. Instead, they can spend their free time, emotions, and money doing things they love!

When you don't have a significant number of items to look after, you can really feel free! You no longer have to account for so many items, which means you can literally do anything. If you want to move to a new city, state, or even country, you don't have to worry about moving vehicles or packing. Instead, you can fit everything in a suitcase, or a couple of suitcases and just go! You don't have to feel like you have to return home for your stuff, or anything at all! Instead, you can demand your life.

Having a lot of stuff and being in the "rat race" to get more can be exhausting. You can get lost in the feeling like you have to work more to get more stuff, which means you're constantly working and never enjoying yourself. You can also get lost in the constant need to clean and maintain all of your belongings. All of this together can really take up all of your time!

10.3 Avoid falling back into old habits

As so much of the modern world is based around consumerist culture, it is important to understand that, as a minimalist, you will constantly be bombarded with advertising designed to make you go against your beliefs. As such, it is important to do everything in your power in order to avoid falling back into bad habits.

1. *Keep your eye on the goal:* Look back to how badly your life was affected by materialism and one thing that does enthuse clients of mine to keep to their new lifestyle is taking photographs of their cluttered lives and then taking new photos of the minimalist lifestyle. These should be enough to remind you of how you became a slave to things and allowed those things to take priority over your happiness, your ability to see beyond these things and have an impact on your spiritual and moral self.

2. *Say positive things each day about the lifestyle that you have chosen:* Let the light into your home and never look back because it's easy to keep to this lifestyle because it is so user friendly. You don't have to waste so much of your life on housework and being a slave to material demands. You don't let life dictate what makes you happy. You have realized that looking back at the way you were and comparing it with how you are now, you get a clear picture of the contrasts. Personal happiness and satisfaction will always win over the confusion of mixed messages caused by materialism.

3. *Try affirmations and mantras:* Affirmations or mantras, positive sentences which are repeated throughout the day, are a great way to ensure that you stay on the straight and narrow. Affirmations are written down while mantras are repeated either aloud or in your head and both

make it easier to block out any negative static that your fixed mindset has to contribute in a given situation.

Common mantras and affirmations include things like:
- I can follow my path to happiness no matter how rocky it may be
- Success is measured in forwarding progress
- Through hard work, I can attract the love and success I deserve
- I am strong enough to overcome any obstacle
- I can find fulfilment through dedication and perseverance

To ensure you don't bite off more than you can chew all at once, it is recommended that you start off with an affirmation or mantra that is fairly close to your current mental comfort zone. Starting with something small will make it easier to rewire your brain in a positive direction when compared to starting with something serious right off the bat.

When using mantras and affirmations for the first time it is common for your fixed mindset to actively rebel against them. This means you may feel stupid for writing or thinking them or feel the urge to give up early on because the activity seems pointless. This is just all of the negative filters in your mind trying to do their job and keep you doing whatever it is that you have been doing. While it will be difficult to appreciate in the moment, the fact that they are acting up really just means that they are working which means you should really be pleased as opposed to annoyed. Instead it is important to keep in mind that success will not appear overnight as it will take time for your new and improved mindset to stick. You should feel as though it is easier to keep it up as you go along, however, which should be a fine indicator of your success overall.

If you find that your mindset is more fixed than most and your best efforts don't seem to be making a dent in your negative mentality then you may be trying to make too big of a change all at once. If this is the case then your mantras and affirmations may not be getting through to your psyche regardless of how frequently you use them. If you feel as though this might be the case with you then you may want to dial back the overall positivity of your statements until your brain starts to get the hang of things. Starting with a mild change should be enough to grease the wheels of progress and help you ultimately build to something that can generate serious results.

Once you banish your negative thoughts it will be time to replace them with positive alternatives instead. It is important to have a general idea of what these will be from the start to ensure you don't fill the void with something that ends up being on par, or worse, than what you are replacing.

To get started all you need to do is look inside yourself and consider what exactly you want the end result to be. Once you know what this goal is, the next thing you are going to need to do is ask yourself why you want to make the change in question and how it is going to benefit you in both the short and the long-term. You should strive to always have a larger purpose in mind when setting these goals as it will be far easier to follow through even when the going gets tough.

When you get ready to make a change of this magnitude it is vital that you understand that much of the journey is going to be uphill and the progress will be very slow going. While working towards your goals it is thus crucial to take note of the triggers you were dealing with during your fixed mindset days in order to ensure they don't follow you to your growth mindset phase and end up negating all of your hard work before you even get started. As long as you are aware of what these triggers are then you should be able to successfully avoid them.

4. *Fully commit:* In order to ever hope to see results, you are going to need to dedicate yourself to the idea completely, this means following through without reservation to ensure that your day to day reactions are always on message with what it is that you are striving towards. Making a decision to commit fully to the task at hand will go a long way towards silencing your inner critic. If you don't commit fully, you then ultimately run the risk of falling back into negative habits after months, or even years, and destroying all your hard work.

5. *Understand your triggers:* When it comes to maintaining successfully, it is important to keep in mind are the things that might make you lose control and revert to your bad habits. Understanding your triggers will then help you to understand the habits that they prop up which will make them easier to avoid in the future.

While you may not be able to think of many of your triggers right off the bat, if you go throughout your week and make a list of every time you did something that was actively against your currently stated goal of the moment then you will be on the right track. You will then want to consider what it is that you have come up with and how you can go about mitigating those triggers, at least until you have gotten the concept of self-discipline under control.

Once you have chosen a mantra or affirmation that is right for you, it is important that you utilize it to the fullest. This means you will want to ensure that it is the first thing you think in the morning when you wake up, and then once and hour, on the hour, throughout the rest of the day, before making sure it is the last thing you think before you fall asleep at night. When working through it, ensure that you really focus on the words, to the exclusion of all else.

Your Quick Start Action Step: Don't Go Alone

Starting any major life journey on your own will always prove to be more difficult than if you have someone there cheering you on! The minimalist community is amazing and can be extremely helpful to on the days in which you find it difficult to look past the process of decluttering to a future filled with more time, more money, and more attention for the people you love.

Chapter 11:
Taking it to the Next Level with a Tiny House

Chapter 11: Taking it to the Next Level With a Tiny House
10.1 How Tiny is Tiny?

A new trend has arisen, known as tiny house living. It is a great example of minimalism, because with this type of living, you have to have the minimal amount of stuff, because you do not have the space to have a lot of stuff. You also get really close to your family as well, because you have to learn how to coexist in less than eight hundred square feet of space. This new trend has come about due to some states making tiny houses to give to the homeless that live there, so that they have a place to live, a place they can call their own.

Once people saw that you can live comfortably in a really small house if it is built right, they wanted to reduce their living space, and give it a try. There are so many options for tiny house living, and some options are really simple, such as living in a camper. Some people have a tiny house built for them as well, and these ones are a lot more complex than just living in a camper.

Tiny house living is a trend where people live in a dwelling that is less than eight hundred square feet of space. Some people argue that it has become even smaller, and to be considered a tiny house it has to be less than five hundred square feet of space. These people are known as extremists. Because a family of five would have a hard time squeezing into anything less than seven hundred square feet. However, if you are a smaller family, then it is generally not considered tiny house living until you reach five hundred or less.

There are many different ways to do tiny house living. Some people get a small camper, and they live in it. A camper is great if you want to be mobile and travel the world, or even if you just want to cut down on utility bills, because most campsites will cut you a good deal if you live there year round. Most campsites you can get a deal where if you pay up front for the whole month, it is only 200 dollars a month. Or, better yet, you can get a job as a camp host and live there year round for free. Living in a camper is not that bad, as you have a bathroom in most, a kitchen, beds, a table and a living space where you can put up a television.

Often times, the kitchen table and the couch in the living area also turn into beds, so you have extra sleeping space. You can get close to nature, and you can sure save a lot of money, especially if you become a camp host. You can't have a whole lot of stuff either, because there just is not space for it, which makes it great for minimalism.

You could turn a shed into a tiny house. This is what a lot of people do, as they find sheds are pretty cheap to purchase, and it doesn't take much to get them up to code. You can even find sheds already wired and ready for electricity, all you have to do is add plumbing, which for such a small space would not take a lot of money, because with a tiny space like that it is ideal to have the bathroom and the kitchen ran on the same wall. You can find sheds that have porches and doors like a little house, and some even come with lofts already built in for your bedroom. It is almost as if these sheds were built for tiny house living, when in reality they used to be used for little shops or play houses for kids. Another good thing about these sheds is that they are easily moved, and you can even make them mobile on their own by welding an old trailer frame to them and adding wheels. Then you can travel with it as if it were a camper. The great thing about these tiny sheds is that you can install solar panels on them for fairly cheap if you make them yourself, and it does not take many to power the entire place.

Another option is to build your own tiny home. This has some downsides and some upsides. The downside is, most of the time if you build your own, it has to be stationary due to coding reasons in most states. You cannot make it mobile, so you would have to find a space to settle down and build there. Another downside is it can be kind of expensive if you add a lot of amenities to your tiny house, such as sliding walls to make it seem like you have more space because when you aren't using the kitchen, you can just slide it into the wall, same with the bath room and bedrooms. The upsides are plenty though.

You can make the house just as you want it, so you know you are getting the most out of the space that you have. You can make it the most energy efficient possible.

This is a good thing, because you can save money on utilities. You can even completely remove your need for electricity if you use solar panels. So then you would only have to pay the city for sewage, water and trash. Plus you can make your tiny house entirely electric so you won't need a gas bill either. This can save you over two hundred dollars a month on utilities alone. Plus if you keep the bill down on building your tiny home, then you can save money that way as well.

You can also buy pre-made tiny homes. There are ones that are built into the ground, and they are called hobbit homes. They get their design from the home that Bilbo Baggins lives in in the Hobbit trilogy. You can plant a garden on top of your home, and they are completely reliant on renewable energy. You can also buy tiny homes that look like tiny homes. These tiny homes also are generally installed with solar panels, and they can be put wherever you like. These too are meant to be stationary though, so you have to be sure of where you want to live.

10.2 Why People Choose Tiny Living

There are many different reasons to choose living in a tiny home. A lot of people find it comforting to be so close to their family, and to have a space that is cozy. Here are the benefits to living in a tiny house.

1. *Less Stuff:* Living in a tiny home makes it impossible to accumulate a lot of stuff. You have to make sure that everything you have you absolutely need, because if you do not need it, it will just clutter up your little home, so to avoid clutter, you get rid of a lot of your stuff. This helps you shift your focus to your family, and away from devices that you really don't need.
2. *Closeness:* Think about your family now. When was the last time your kids came to you for advice? Which parent do they bother more? Do they talk to either parent really at all? When was the last time everyone sat down to dinner and talked about their day? With tiny house living, you have to communicate with your family because you are all pretty much on top of each other twenty four/seven. This is great for when your kids hit their

teenage years, because they cannot run off and shut themselves in their rooms and ignore the world. They have to come to you for advice.

If they have lived the tiny house lifestyles most of their life, they will end up wanting to come to you for advice, because they will be use to the closeness you all share as a family. This will create a bond between you and your children and help them grow up and turn into secure adults, because they will know for sure that you are there for them. Sure, in the beginning going from a large space to a tiny one can be aggravating, but if you stick with it, you will begin to love the fact that you are in the same room with your family all day, because it opens the gates of communication. Think about it. How awkward would it be to sit in the same room with them day in and day out in silence? Pretty awkward. So you are forced to communicate, and eventually the house will be filled with laughter and joy.

3. *Simplicity:* There is something amazing about just sitting back and enjoying life, not worried about having a whole huge house to clean. Life is a whole lot easier when it only takes twenty minutes to clean the entire house. You also find that you get in a better routine of picking things up in order to keep your sanity in check, because tiny houses get cluttered easily. Life is easier in a tiny house, and in some ways, it is a lot better.

10.3 How Tiny Houses Equal Minimalism

Tiny houses are a type of minimalism to be honest. You are minimizing everything, including your living space. Think about it. You can't have a lot of junk if you have nowhere to store it. In a tiny house you have to have the minimum of everything, from clothes, to dishes. Everything has to be taken in moderation. That is what minimalism is. Less is more, and you can get along just fine without all the gadgets and gizmos that the world says you have to have.

Tiny house living is a great form of minimalism because it is tangible minimalism. You actually feel that you are living the lifestyles, rather than just following some guidelines, and this is a great thing, because it can make you want to spread the word all over the world. This is an amazing feeling and can spread like the flu to others as well.

Think about it. You are moving from a house that is probably over a thousand square feet into something that is less than five hundred square feet. That is a big difference. You are going from a large dining room table, a roomy living room with a large recliner, long couch, and a love seat all around a large flat screen television. To a room that houses your living, dining, and cooking space. You leave behind a giant refrigerator and downsize to a small apartment sized or smaller refrigerator. You go from having enough dishes to serve a small army to having just enough dishes to serve your family. You downsize on clothes, keeping only what you wear on a regular basis, and getting rid of all of the rest. You go from having kitchen gadgets galore, to only having a stove, and maybe a toaster and microwave.

You get rid of anything you do not absolutely need. You go from a house full of stuff, most of which you haven't messed with in months or more, to the bare necessities. Not much more than a bed, the clothes on your back, and the food in your stomach. Everything else goes. Yet, you will find, that you couldn't be happier, because you are away from the stress of having too much stuff.

Your Quick Start Action Step: Don't Go Alone
When was the last time you went camping? How did it make you feel? Chances are, you felt at peace, and you never wanted to leave. That is because you were experiencing a small dose of minimalism, and just that small dose was enough to leave you wanting more. Minimalism does work, and tiny house living is a lot like permanent camping. You may find that you never want to live in a large house again.

Bonus Chapter: Getting Rid of Digital Clutter to Maximize Technology Use and Simplifying Your Life

Bonus Chapter: Getting Rid of Digital Clutter to Maximize Technology Use and Simplifying Your Life

12.1 Know your enemy

Digital clutter is a sneaky thing. Unlike the surplus gadgets in your kitchen, data hides on your computer, your smartphone, and in the cloud. It also festers within your credit card purchase history, schoolwork, medical records, driver's abstract, and any legal proceedings you've been party to. Yet much of this information is largely invisible. Sure, you walk by your computer daily or pick up your smartphone frequently but the information within is in a nice
tidy package. Only when you start looking for something specific are you likely to realize that you have too many emails, digital photographs, or other files. The volume and variety of information can be a burden in ways you might not even realize.

Whether you like it or not, digital clutter is inevitable. Only the most diligent have taken time to be rigorous about deleting old files, organizing current files, and so on. More often the solution is to buy more storage to house an ever growing data collection. This chapter will explore the kinds of data in your life, and strategies to help you manage your information. Think of it as a digital cleanse.

Digital decluttering is the process of organizing your data and technology in ways that support your lifestyle. To get started, you need to be clear on what digital clutter is and why decluttering is important to you. In this part, we'll explore the digital clutter problem, the benefits of digital decluttering, and how the process works.

Online technologies have evolved and changed our lives at home and in the office at a dramatic pace over the past 30 years. The rate at which we've adopted new technologies and improvements to Internet upload and download speeds are impressive. Add to that the evolution from pagers to smartphones and the increased power of the computer for even more change.

However, all that change has created a problem: Digital clutter.
Before we dive in, it may be helpful to pause a moment and consider what digital cluttering means to you. How do you define it? How does digital clutter make you feel? How does it impact your life?

Digital clutter is a fairly new problem. Our ancestors may have lived with too many objects but they didn't live with the same volume of information. By ancestors, we only have to look one generation back. Some grew up with analog information and have had to adapt to digital living while others were born into the digital life. For both groups, digital clutter is an artifact of the Internet, personal computers, social networking, and smart devices. We now consciously create and unconsciously contribute to terabytes of data every year.

Our personal collection of data started slowly. With home and office computers, work previously done by hand or with typewriters and adding machines moved into word processing and spreadsheet software. Files were stored on floppy disks and rudimentary hard drives. In 1993, there were about 600 websites. Early Internet adopters may have accessed those first websites, a few Bulletin
Board System (BBS) message boards and, possibly, had an ICQ
identity. I seek you, remember?

Flash forward and today we live with what too much data smog
We have millions of websites and years' worth of YouTube videos to watch plus social networking and cloud storage. Add to that our mobile phones, tablets, laptops, and smart home devices. We have vast search histories and medical, financial, and shopping digital records. And let's not forget any lingering remnants of data from our older collections of USB drives, SD cards, and defunct computers. Think back to when you first started using a computer. How much data have you created since then? How much information have you accessed?

To quantify that data think in terabytes (TB). You know, bytes, kilobytes, megabytes, gigabytes, terabytes, and so on. The Register recently quoted a Western Digital Corporation finding that the "average US household has 41.5 TB of data spread across 14 digital devices, and this is only going to grow"

That 41.5 TB can hold more than 1 million hours of 1080 HD video or nearly 21 million digital photos of 2 MB each or trillions of pages of text. That's just the average per household!

Unfortunately, we spend a lot of our time just clearing the junk, which we're now forced to do in order to discover anything we might actually care about. By sheer volume alone, everyone needs to do some data decluttering.

12.2 Benefits of Digital Decluttering

No matter its origins, digital information is central to our way of living today. As a result, we've got to take ownership of our digital footprint. Beyond simply clearing the clutter, there are many benefits.

Better organization means efficiency and, if time is money, it improves your bottom line. By knowing what information you have and where to find it, you can make the most of your time both online and offline. In doing so, you reduce the amount of information you have to process — what psychologists call "cognitive load"— and self-administer the antidote to information overwhelm.

That recovered time and reduced cognitive load can be used to nurture your interests and try new things. Furthermore, reducing the digital noise around you minimizes distractions and creates space to focus on more complex projects, including analog projects away from your computer.

Digital decluttering also creates space for self-care. Taking control of the amount of time you spend online allows you to focus on what's important to you. Time away from the screen is the best prevention for "sitting disease," a term I first heard from the pelvic health specialist, Kim Vopni. Less screen time can also improve your sleep patterns, protect your hearing, and give your eyes a much needed rest.

That same self-care space allows you to nourish meaningful relationships, reigniting your listening skills and ability to focus. Genuine connections are often lost in the digital clutter and rekindling the skills to foster those connections benefit all. If you're a parent or other role model for children and youth, demonstrating the healthy use of technology is one of the best ways to pass on this digital life lesson.

In addition to the practical, physical, and social benefits of digital decluttering, you may find peace in other aspects of your life. Understanding your data and how you use technology can highlight the myths of the perfectly polished life. What is published online is often a curated collection of posts that perpetuate the myth of the perfect life. Knowing this can reduce envy and your need to
"keep up with the Joneses."

Similarly, understanding your data can help you find the elements that are key in your quest for digital happiness. If you love taking photographs, then take photographs! If Instagram Stories make you happy, then create and view them. However, you should strive to put strategies in place to put boundaries around your use of technology so that the digital parts of your life are fulfilling, not draining.

Digital decluttering can also be a good reminder of the privilege of digital access. Not all sectors of society nor all places in the world have such ready access to technology and information. By noting this privilege, we can be appreciative of the opportunity rather than burdened by the requirements of digital living. This awareness can also complement the trend towards minimalism.

Digital decluttering also allows you to prepare your digital legacy. Long after you've passed away, your information will still be available. It's not easy to think about our own mortality but it has become an essential part of estate planning. While alive, you get to decide what information you leave behind and who will have access to it after you're gone. If you don't make arrangements in advance, some data may become inaccessible and other data might be used in undesirable ways.

As you can see, the time invested in digital decluttering has many benefits. I consider myself an advocate for living an integrated digital life that includes both digital and analog components. An integrated digital life includes the mindful use of technology to achieve your goals. You choose what devices you have and how you use them. And, whenever possible, use the power you have to decide what data you create and what data you keep.

12.3 Free Yourself from Unwanted Files

1. *Start with the easy stuff:* Go through your computer's files. Discard the ones you don't want or need. Then empty the trash can or recycle bin so you can't go back and retrieve them later. Use the rule of 12. If you haven't used the file for 12 or more months, you probably don't need it. If it is an important file, like a bill, medical information, or tax forms, put it in a folder labeled "Important Documents" and leave it on your computer where you can access the files at any time.

2. *Manage Your Media:* File your music, photos, and other media in the appropriate folders. Make them easy to find by keeping them on your desktop where they can be easily seen. You can keep your desktop clutter

free by making a master media folder and then creating sub folders for the different media formats. Just like with your files, go through and delete any media you don't want or need to keep anymore. Deleting the unwanted files will free up space on your hard drive and give you the ability to download other media in the future.

3. *Pick Your Programs:* Did you download Picasso thinking you were going to edit all your vacation pictures, but then forgot to do it? Uninstall the programs you don't use anymore. This will help speed up your computer and reduce the risk of you having potentially malware targeted software taking up space on your hard drive.

4. *Strengthen and Store Your Passwords:* Review all your passwords. Strengthen and change them as you see fit. Make sure all your passwords are unique and use letters (Upper and Lower Case) and numbers. If you have a lot of passwords to remember download and use a password manager. Password managers help you by remembering all your passwords so that you don't have to.

5. *Back That Data Up:* Ideally, you are backing up your important data all the time. However, if you haven't done it in a while...or ever, consider doing it now. Use a portable hard drive or cloud service to make sure that your files exist in a place outside of your home or office. This will ensure that if anything happens to your computer like it crashes or implodes, you won't lose all your data.

6. *Reinstall Your Operating System:* Once you have successfully backed up all your data you might consider reinstalling your operating system. While it may not seem necessary with modern technology, it is always nice to start fresh. Reinstalling has the potential to speed up your computer. Not

sure how to reinstall? Just do a google search for "How to reinstall Windows/MAC (insert version here)."

7. *Set-Up Internet Security:* You should get an antivirus, anti-phishing and anti-spyware software as well as a firewall. If you already have them simply perform updates to make sure they are running at their optimum level. If you don't, do your research and choose software the will best meet your needs. If you want to add an extra layer of security you can get a VPN (Virtual Private Network) for the time you use free Wi-Fi. Try ProXPN for free and see what all the VPN hype is about.

8. *Refresh Your Phone:* Go through all your devices and perform system updates. Then review and delete any unwanted apps to free up space. Use that free space to download a security app for your phone. These apps can help ensure that no one is hacking into your phone's data. Both iPhone and Android users can try Lookout for free in the app store or on Google Play.

Do these 8 tasks and eliminate the digital clutter from your life. Making it a priority to organize your digital life will help give you peace of mind. So in-between dusting the ceiling fans and shampooing the carpets, take a few minutes to clean up your digital clutter. Trust us, you will be glad you did!

Your Quick Start Action Step: Start by making it searchable
Digital clutter doesn't always need to be "organized," and it mostly doesn't need frequent cleaning, with the possible exception of if someone else is going to be sharing it. It does need to be searchable, however, so you can find what you want when you want it and that you know what you have for when you are ultimately ready to get rid of the junk. Judicious use of tags, titles, and keywords can help.

Conclusion

Thank you again for owning this book!

I hope it was able to help you to achieve your personal mental decluttering goals, whatever it is that they may be. Just because you've finished this book doesn't mean there is nothing left to learn on the topic, and expanding your horizons is the only way to find the mastery you seek. The next step is to stop reading already and to get ready to get started cleaning the mental clutter from your mind once and for all.

While you are no doubt anxious to get started, it is important to do so with realistic expectations in mind, especially if you feel as though you have been hanging on to mental clutter for quite some time. While the human brain is certainly capable of developing new ways of looking at the world, these sorts of things take time. In fact, depending on the amount of clutter you are dealing with, it could take weeks or even months of hard work before you start seeing results. It is important to not lose faith in the interim, however, as you will only find the success you seek if you keep up the good work. As such, it is best to think of decluttering your mind as a marathon, not a sprint, which means that slow and steady wins the race.

Thank you and good luck!

Preview Of 'Minimalist Budget' by Marie S. Davenport

Chapter 6 – Dealing with Debt

6.1

The simplest way to describe debt is money that is owed from one party to the other. It may get complicated quickly. It all depends on the amount of debt you have and the way you handle it. Debt can be a useful tool or baggage that complicates your life.

Knowing the right way to handle debt can be difficult especially if you constantly struggle to cover your monthly bills. There are various ways to handle each type of debt. There are also ways to get relief from debt. Just be careful of companies that sound too good to be true or promise you absurd things. Here are the two most common types of debt and ways to handle them:

- **Secured debt**: A secured debt is one where the borrower has provided some asset as collateral to secure the loan. Mortgages and car loans are examples of a secured debt. If you don't pay, the creditor can take the said asset like foreclosing your house or repossessing your car.

- **Unsecured debt** is never backed by an asset. One example is a credit card. This doesn't mean you won't have consequences if you don't pay your bills. The creditor can sell your debt to a collection agency that will then call you night and day for payment. If you still don't pay, they might be able to sue you for payment. This might lead to your wages being garnished. Some creditors might sue you without using a collection agency.

6.2

Most people wonder how much of their money is theirs and the amount they pay toward debt factors in on how their debt is accumulated. There are many reasons why we have debt, such as unemployment or unforeseen emergencies. More often than not, debt is caused by bad spending habits. If you aren't paying with cash, it will cost you to spend money.

Think about a credit card being somebody who is granting you a favor to buy things you cannot afford but will let you pay them off later. Actually, the truth is you just wind up owing more and not getting everything you need.

Everybody alive tries to keep up with their neighbors. They have the life we've always wished for, and we will never be able to keep up with them. These things we long for lead us to huge amounts of debt. When we don't know how to manage this debt, it can cause our credit card bills to grow endlessly.

Let's look at making a purchase of $500 without a credit card. You think this is a good deal because you only have to pay $15 a month. This is very manageable for you. What you don't realize is the creditor is adding an additional $147 to that bill for interest. If you only pay $15 each month, it is going to take you four years to pay off that $500 charge. That is assuming you have an interest rate of 14.7 percent. If your credit card has a higher interest rate, this purchase at 22 percent means you are going to be paying out an additional $280 in interest. Yes, you still have those four years to pay off a total of $780, so is that item worth that much more?

If you add in all our wants with the large investments of cars and homes along with the planned necessities like weddings and college as well as the unplanned emergencies like relocation, unemployment, and medical emergencies, it is easy to visualize how quickly debt can grow. The main reason people get into debt is a combination of personal and impersonal finances.

6.3

Even if your debt is small, you have to manage it well. You have to make your payments on time and be sure it doesn't get out of hand. If your debt is large, you must put in more effort to pay it off while making your other payments.

1. **Know your creditors and the amounts you owe.**

    Create a list of debts that include the creditor, complete amount you owe, how much your payments are, and when they are due. Use a credit report to confirm your debts. Having the debts in front of you lets you see the bigger picture, so you are aware of your whole debt. Don't make a list and then forget about it. Look at it from time to time, especially when you pay your bills. Update the list every month or two when the list changes.

2. **Pay your dues on time.**

    Making late payments will make it harder for you to pay off the debt because you are going to have to pay an extra late fee for each payment you miss. If you miss two payments, your finance charges and interest rate will go up. If you use a calendar, place your payments and set an alarm to give you an alert a couple days before the payment needs to be made. If you miss a payment, don't wait until it becomes due again. The creditor may report it to a credit bureau. Make your payment once you remember.

3. **Make a bill-paying calendar.**

   Use a calendar to help you figure out what bill to pay with a certain paycheck. Write every bill's payment on the day it is due. Next, put in the calendar when you get paid. If you get paid on the same date, this is an easy step for you. If your paychecks come on a different day, it will help to make a note each month.

4. **Always make your minimum payment.**

   If the minimum amount is all you can pay, that is fine—just do it on time. This isn't going to get you any progress in paying off your debt. It will keep the debt from growing and will keep your account good. If you miss a payment, it becomes harder to get caught up. Your account may go into default.

5. **Figure out what debt you need to pay off fastest.**

   Paying off any credit card debt first is the best strategy since these have higher interest rates. It must be the priority since it will cost you the most money. Use your list of debts, and rank them in order that you want to pay them off. You may also choose to pay off the one with the lowest balance first.

6. **Pay off any charge-offs and collections.**

   You can only pay what you can afford. If you have limited funds to repay debts, try to focus on keeping other accounts in good standing. Never sacrifice good accounts for ones that have already changed your credit. Pay the past due accounts when you can afford them. These creditors are going to keep hounding you for payment until it is brought current.

7. **Have an emergency fund to help out in hard situations.**

    You may have to go into debt to cover an emergency if you don't want to dip into your savings account. A small emergency fund can cover small expenses that may pop up now and then. Begin by working to create a small fund. An amount of $ 1,000 is a great place to start. When you have that amount, try to increase it to another thousand. You want to try to create a reserve that equals your six months' pay.

8. **Create a monthly budget to plan expenses.**

    Keeping a budget will help you make sure that you have the money to cover all expenses each month. Plan in advance so that you can take action if you are going to be short one month. Budgets help you plan how to use any extra money you may have left after all expenses have been paid. You may have enough money to pay another debt off.

9. **See the signs that you are in need of help.**

    If you see that it is too hard for you to pay your bills and debts every month, you can turn to a debt relief company for help. Check out credit counseling agencies in your area. Other options are bankruptcy, debt settlement, and debt consolidation. All of these have disadvantages and advantages, so check each option carefully. If you have a spending problem, you can seek help through a Debtors Anonymous group. This is similar to Alcoholics Anonymous.

10. **Change Your Debt Like Behaviors**

    In order to get out of debt, you have to eliminate the reasons you may up in debt in the first place. Even winning the Powerball Jackpot won't fix your problem if you don't learn how to spend less than what you make.

Everybody has their own reasons for winding up in debt. Medical bills, job loss, school, or just plain young stupidity are all widely common reasons. However, the reason you have gotten into debt doesn't matter all that much. What matters the most is that you don't let this happen again. Here are some things you must not do:

- If you have to take out $50k in student loans to get your bachelor's degree, don't take out an extra $100k for a Ph.D.

- Did you end up falling into a large pile of debt when you lost your job? Resolve, after you have gotten out of debt, to work on building up an emergency fund so that you won't have to face this problem again.

- If you spend several years living a life that you can't afford, then you have to figure out the life that you can actually afford, and get to that point.

That last point is a lot easier said than done. The truth is that the last point is the main reason for this book and about a third of all financial articles you can find online. Let's be honest: how many articles have you seen that are labeled, "Live within your means," "Spend less than your monthly income," and so on? Why has there been so much stuff written on this very simple concept?

This is because after a person has gotten used to living in a certain way, it is extremely hard to change that habit. It will be like having to live on ramen after living for two years on The Capital Grille.

11. When to Refinance or Consolidate

Two of the most common things people do when faced with a lot of debt is consolidation and refinancing. Consolidation means that you put all of your debts into one loan. This will help you by allowing you to deal with only one lender. This means you won't be faced with several different monthly billing statements.

Refinancing means that you replace all of your old debts with a new loan. The goal of doing this is to get a lower interest rate. The majority of students will use consolidation for their student loans. This works if all of the debts are from a government program.

There are many different online calculators to help you figure out if refinancing works for you and to make sure that you pick the best one. Before you decide to consolidate or refinance, take the following into consideration:

- Has your credit score gone up any? This will place you in a favorable light with lenders. This means you will be able to start a tangible process of removing all of your old debt with a new lender that offer better terms.

- Do you already have low-interest rates? If this is the case, you can take advantage of it. Change your variable rate to a fixed rate.

- Are you able to change your payment terms? Dragging your debt along with you for a long time won't help you to become debt-free. If you are making more money and can afford it, start making larger payments each month.

Your Quick Start Action Step:

You are not alone in your debt. Most people in the world are also in debt. If you live in denial, it will only increase your money problems along with your anxiety. When you can face your situation, paying off those debts may be easier than you realize.

- Fast facts: The first thing you have to do is to figure out how big your problem is. Start by looking at your last bank statement and finding any missing paperwork. Open bills you have been neglecting. Create a list of the amount you owe every company and their interest rates. When you have figured out this information, you will begin to prioritize all your debts.

- Transfer to a zero-percent credit card. If you have expensive credit cards, see if you can transfer the debt to a zero-percent credit card. These cards can eliminate interest charges for a certain period. This makes sure that every cent you repay will go toward paying down your balance. In order to get the most out of these cards, you need to pay off the balance in the offer window. If you know you can't repay the whole amount in the introductory period, look for low-interest rate cards. You are still going to pay interest every month, but it will be at a low rate. These types of cards require an unblemished credit score.

- Think about overdraft options. If you pay a lot of interest in overdraft fees, this can quickly accelerate your debt problems. If you think you may be paying too much for your overdraft service, see if your bank has a different account you can switch to, or drop the overdraft from your account entirely.

- You may consider a personal loan. There may be a time when getting a personal loan can help you manage your debt. Find a leading market rate with the APR lower than what you are currently paying on your credit card. If you look around, it may be possible to find a rate lower than eight percent. This is a lot better than the normal 17 to 22 percent that normal credit cards charge. If you need to borrow a large sum of money, a personal loan is a way to go. Larger loans usually come with lower APRs than those with smaller amounts. Don't borrow more money than you need since this may increase your chances of getting deeper into debt. Always shop around. You aren't going to get a good rate if you accept the first offer from the first lender you go to.

Chapter 7 – Overall Budget Techniques Applied to Daily, Monthly, and Long-Term Expenses

7.1

We've used the word budget and budgeting a lot throughout this book. While it may sound like a bad word to many, especially for those who know how taking a deeper look at their finances is going to reveal some pretty bad habits that they would rather stay hidden, it is an extremely helpful tool when it comes to a minimalist budget.

Budgeting is known to be difficult, even when it comes to just keeping track of where all of your money goes. The first question people will ask you is if you are trying to budget before taxes (i.e. gross income) or after taxes (i.e. net income)?

If you want to begin with your gross income, it will be best to look at the percentage that is saved in your 401(k). If your company offers you a match offer, make sure you put away enough to get it. The maximum contribution of an employee for a 401(k) is $18,000 in 2016, so try not to go over this limit. However, this does not include what your employer will contribute. The limit for you and your employer's contribution is $53,000. You can also have health insurance premiums that are automatically deducted from your pay if your company provides you insurance, so there is a chance that you won't have to include this into your post-tax budget.

After you have become comfortable with how your payroll and pre-tax deduction saving works, you can then focus on your budget for net income, which is what most people look at day-to-day. If you plan on being really minimalist with your budget, here is a suggestion: the 65-25-10 rule.

- 65% is spent on your day-to-day living.
- 25% is spent on large expenses and retirement, including emergencies.
- 10% is given away to your favorite causes or charity.

You can get really nitty-gritty about it, and break them down even further. However, when you are trying to see the big picture, sometimes it's good just to have a few numbers. If you have to provide your own savings, then you may want the breakdown to be 65-15-10-10.

- 65% is still day-to-day expenses.
- 15% is your emergency and large expenses.
- 10% is retirement expenses.
- 10% is charity expenses.

The hard decisions are made in the day-to-day expenses. If you make sure that you automate your savings money and set them aside, you will make sure that you won't spend the amount that you intended to save on eating out or impulse buys because the money won't be in your checking account.

When you are first starting out with budgeting, or when you are trying to get a handle on your spending, try using a cash-only method or limit yourself a lot when it comes to using your credit card. If you do use a credit card, start going in and manually categorizing and entering your purchases so that you will become aware of the things you are spending.

Much like how you log your calories when you want to lose weight, typing in each dollar you spend into a spreadsheet will help you to become more aware of the way you use your money, which is the first step you need to take toward financial success.

After you have gotten a handle on your spending, you can upgrade to a program that will download your credit card and bank information so that you won't have to write everything down by hand, but make sure that you still set aside some time to really look over your weekly spending so that you can see how you are balancing yourself across different categories. If you overspend in one category, that's okay—just try to under-spend in another one.

This budgeting will require a bit of work on your part—but in the end, it will help you save for and spend on the things that are the most important.

To learn more about "Minimalist Budget" by Marie S. Davenport, visit the Amazon website.

Minimalist Budget

*Simple and Practical
Budgeting Strategies to Save Money,
Avoid Compulsive Spending,
Pay Off Debt and Simplify Your Life*

Marie S. Davenport

© **Copyright 2018 by Marie S. Davenport - All rights reserved.**

The contents of this book may not be reproduced, duplicated or transmitted without direct written permission from the author.

Under no circumstances will any legal responsibility or blame be held against the publisher for any reparation, damages, or monetary loss due to the information herein, either directly or indirectly.

Legal Notice:

This book is copyright protected. This is only for personal use. You cannot amend, distribute, sell, use, quote or paraphrase any part or the content within this book without the consent of the author.

Disclaimer Notice:

Please note the information contained within this document is for educational and entertainment purposes only. Every attempt has been made to provide accurate, up to date and reliable complete information. No warranties of any kind are expressed or implied. Readers acknowledge that the author is not engaging in the rendering of legal, financial, medical or professional advice. The content of this book has been derived from various sources. Please consult a licensed professional before attempting any techniques outlined in this book.

By reading this document, the reader agrees that under no circumstances are is the author responsible for any losses, direct or indirect, which are incurred as a result of the use of information contained within this document, including, but not limited to, —errors, omissions, or inaccuracies.

Table of Contents

Introduction

Chapter 1: Getting Started with a Minimalist Budget

Chapter 2: Shifting Your Mindset from Unnecessary Spending and Debt Build-Up to Simple and Smart Spending & Budgeting

Chapter 3: Reviewing Your Personal Finances

Chapter 4: Simplified Financial Planning Goes a Long Way

Chapter 5: Unnecessary Compulsive Spending and How to Fix It

Chapter 6: Dealing with Debt

Chapter 7: Overall Budget Techniques Applied to Daily, Monthly, and Long-Term Expenses

Chapter 8: Recycling the Right Way While Still Making Money

Chapter 9: The "Less is More" Lifestyle for Debt-Free and Stress-Free Living

Bonus Chapter: Tips on Dealing with Large Expenses

Conclusion

Introduction

If you have ever struggled with your monthly budget—to pay your bills, to make ends meet, to get out of debt, or even to dream a life where you can thrive financially—you are not alone. In fact, 80.9% of baby boomers, 79.9% of Gen Xers, and 81.5% of millennials are living with debt. That's 8 out of every 10 people you meet struggling to get the money monster off their back. The good news is that there is hope, and the answer doesn't even begin with your bank account—it begins with your mindset. Modern society trains us to be consumers without limit, and it is no wonder why so many feel helpless when it comes to the health of their finances. No matter what stage of life you are in, it is not too late to overhaul your budget, to make real financial gains, and to start shaping your life with prosperity mindset.

The *Minimalist Budget* addresses the underlying fears and habits that are preventing you from feeling relieved about your finances. The process begins not by attacking your credit cards, student loans, mortgages, or medical bills blindly, but by first discovering that you have more resources than you realize. By changing your mindset from fear to abundance, you can start feeling more powerful and more confident about making the changes that will improve your finances. The simple and straightforward advice here in *Minimalist Budget* will empower you to stop letting your days be dictated by impulse spending, denial budgeting, and despair about your future.

Chapter 1: Getting Started with a Minimalist Budget

Chapter 1: Getting Started with a Minimalist Budget

1.1

What is everybody's first reaction when a bank card application is declined? Embarrassment. We don't want those around us to think that we don't have money. Suze Orman, a financial expert, says that anger, fear, and shame are the most common emotions that surround money.

Everybody believes that money is just about your bank balance. It is, but it is also connected very strongly to emotions. And before you start believing that you are exempted from these emotions, think again.

What is your emotion when you realize that you are at your last penny? Depression, panic, fear, and anger.

There are times when our emotions towards money become so strong that we begin to hate money because we think it is causing all of our problems. Hate is a pretty strong emotion. Money has also been a reason for some people who have tried to commit suicide.

How would you feel if you inherited a large sum of money or won the lottery? You'll feel elated, probably—relieved, no more money problems—even free, or so you think.

A sudden large sum of money changes people. Money gives them a status and makes them feel powerful. Suddenly, they start to have an air of arrogance. Money can also influence the way someone treats those around them. If a homeless person were to walk into a high-end store, chances are somebody is going to shoo them out. If a person that has a nice suit on and drives a BMW walks into the same store, they'll get the red carpet rolled out for them. People respect those that are wealthy. As sad as this may seem, it is true. That's the power of money.

Our views of money often come from our childhood. The way our parents handled money gave us our foundation for the way we handle money now. This is why generational wealth and poverty exist. Poor people impart their money habits to their children. The same goes for wealthy people. Along with this problem is the fact that poor people are unable to further their children's education.

But the truth is: money isn't the problem. The problem comes from the way you approach money, how you handle money, and how you think about money. People who are constantly negative when it comes to money are always going to be plagued by money issues. Those who think that they can control money are the ones that end up becoming successful and further increase their money. Those are the type of people that, instead of complaining about the money they don't have, educate themselves. Financial intelligence is how you grow wealth.

Changing your financial situation will start with changing how you think about money. It is important that you clear out your negative thoughts about money and get rid of blockages.
While you need to examine your feelings about money and become better at managing it, you need to make sure that you don't let it consume you. Money must not become the center of your life because this can be detrimental to your quality of life, family, and health.

This is why a minimalist budget can help. Before I tell you what it is, let's go over what it's not.

It won't teach you how to maximize credit card deals, coupons, rewards, or any other consumer freebie that will require you to open multiple accounts. It won't help you save the most money or make you a frugal person. It will, however, help you simplify your finances so that you will have an easier system to achieve your financial goals.

1.2

You may be asking why a minimalist budget works. It helps you keep your finances simple so that you are able to pay off your bills, add to your savings, and give you the freedom to use the money for fun things. It is also a great place for budgeting novices to start. You don't have to worry about uncertainty—you will have clear action steps, and it will also be able to provide you with your investment, savings, and financial goals. This is the reason why you will be more likely to stick to the plan until you reach your desired goal of financial stability.

A minimalist budget will also give you some flexibility. You are able to bend things a bit so that it works better for you. You don't have to be exact about how things work because budgets will differ from one person to another. The important thing is to take action and make use of a system that helps you remain consistent in managing your monthly income and to make sure that you cover the expenses that you need to. You are responsible for your savings, and you have some wiggle room to enjoy life.

1.3

Now that you have an idea of what a minimalist budget is, let's look at some ways that you can do to start changing your life and improving your finances.

   12. Change the way you view borrowing or payments to owning.

   There are a lot of people who are "broke" that will talk about owning things in terms of payments. They say things like "I got the car because there was a great deal on the lease. My monthly payments are only $200."

Their goals are to stretch out their finances as much as they can so that they can live beyond their means with a lifestyle that they feel entitled to but are not able to afford.

With a minimalist budget, you will be required to flip this kind of view upside-down. Instead of looking at things in terms of payments, you have to view things in terms of ownership. Don't ask about monthly payments; instead, ask what it would cost to buy it outright.

This can be done by believing that your income potential is limitless, not being frugal, and staying away from credit cards. This is very different from the majority of people, but it is the best way to gain financial freedom.

13. **Establish financial priorities, and define financial values.**

To be able to get rid of unnecessary things, you have to figure out what is unnecessary to you. This means that you will have to define everything that is important to you. After you have figured out what you really value the most, you can then come up with financial priorities. Some examples of financial values are:

   a. Retire by the age of 55.
   b. Donate 10% of your income to your favorite charity.
   c. Have a 30% buffer between expenses and income.
   d. Save 20% of your monthly income.
   e. Live debt-free.

After you have decided on what your values are, you will then establish your priorities. These priorities are basically your financial goals. These are your plan for moving from where you are to where you are going to be. These are going to vary based on your current status.

Some examples would be:

1. Come up with a long-term plan that will give you the opportunity to retire at 55.
2. Make 20% more money by doing something on the side.
3. Start to donate 10% to your favorite charity.
4. Once you have repaid all of your debt, start saving 20% of your income.
5. Pay off your debt in three years.

These are only a few examples. There are a lot of things you can do to create your own priorities. When you aren't sure of what you want, following a 50/20/30 budget is a great idea, and we will go into that in chapter seven.

Another thing you need to look at is the value of experience as compared to physical things. Research has found that people are happier when they spend money on experiences instead of spending their money on material things. It's easy for it to feel like buying things is the only way to be happy, especially in American culture. However, this isn't true, so fight that feeling. Start prioritizing experiences over things.

It's extremely important that you figure out your values and define your priorities so that you can come up with a minimalist budget. The foundation of this way of living is prioritizing the things that are important and forgetting all the other things.

14. **Live simply with fewer credit cards and accounts.**

A person with a minimalist budget will normally have one main checking and one main savings account. The checking account is needed for discretionary and non-discretionary expenses. The savings account will be used as an emergency fund.

If you need to have a credit card, only have one. You may give up some rewards, but you will be making your life simpler and making things easier for you to stay organized and on top of your spending.

This is the biggest area where people make mistakes. There are people that own seven-plus savings and checking accounts; one for an emergency, one for down payment, one for taxes, and so on. It gets messy, and normally they will end up borrowing from one to fund another. Then, there are some people who are stuck in payment mode. They have payments going in a million different directions, and they are barely saving anything.

15. **Think twice before you purchase.**

When you have a minimalist budget, you have to question all of your purchases. Ask yourself if it is absolutely necessary. Keep in mind that it will take some time for you to earn money, so all of your purchases need to be worth the time you spent making that money.

16. **Schedule financial meetings.**

It's one thing to organize your finances and to have a plan; it's another thing to implement it. There are some things in your life that are going to change and will make your plan unworkable.

It's important that you review, revise, and evaluate your budget regularly to keep things working. Set a monthly financial meeting with yourself and with your spouse if you have one. This gives you time to change your budget.

17. Be okay with feeling like a weirdo.

Others may think that you are being completely weird, so get used to it. What you're doing is a good thing. You are living intentionally, and you have a plan for your money. A lot of people don't do this, and if they judge you, it's just because they don't understand it.

18. Keep Up with Your Spending for the Previous Month

Figuring out just where all of your money has gone during the past month is going to be one of the longest and time-consuming things you will have to do. Luckily, this will only have to be done once a month, so suck it up and get on with it. Gather up all of your bank statements, receipts, and credit card statements from the previous month. Now, you need to come up with budget categories and then match up your spending.

If this doesn't seem like something that you want to do by hand, there are plenty of online money management tools that can help you do this. Some of the budget categories that you must create include:

- Savings
- Debt payments – student loans, car loans, credit cards, and so on.
- Insurance
- Living expenses – utilities, rent, and the like
- Entertainment
- Food
- Miscellaneous

In later chapters, we will go further in depth on all of these different categories that you will have to figure out.

19. Give your Money a New Direction

Hopefully, you have a pretty good goal that will help you stay motivated with your new minimalist budget. This will help you go full-force into redirecting your money. Once you have taken a good look at your spending patterns, you must have a pretty good idea as to where all of your money is going—so now, how much do you have left to spend once you reach the end of the month?

If there isn't any extra money to spend, then you will have to cut back on some of your spendings. When you make these cuts, you need to make sure that you are realistic. If you know that you are going to spend $50 on gas each week, then don't choose that area to cut back. This is only going to be setting yourself up for failure.

Instead, choose areas to cut back on that will be less painful. This can mean groceries. You may be spending too much money on entertainment things. You must never cut back on your debt repayments, but all of the other categories can and must be cut back on if at all possible.

Your Quick Start Action Step:

To help you get started on this right now, here are few quick action steps that you can start doing right this minute.

20. Come up with a list of your spending, and evaluate your consumption.

Come up with a list of everything that you spend your money on. The more detailed you can make this, the better it will be. After you have created your list, evaluate every item. Ask if that item adds something meaningful to your life. Do you value the item? Does it help you achieve your priorities and values?

Keep in mind that when you say yes to something, you will be saying no to something else. When you say yes to something that adds no value, you are saying no to yourself.

Let's assume that you spend $150 every month on your hair. Ask yourself if spending this is serving your end priorities and values. If it isn't helping you in that manner, is it something that you find more important than your future? You can say yes, or you can say no. The important thing to understand is that when you spend this money on certain stuff, you have to eliminate spending elsewhere.

When you find that you are spending money on things that aren't in line with your financial future, you need to cut out those expenses.

21. **Come up with a spending plan.**

This involves listing out your expenses and comparing them to your income. This is where you need to break down your expenses and income and figure out where you want to spend your money. Everybody has different expenses, so this is a personal thing that you have to come up with.

22. **Automate payments.**

Since minimalism involves making your finances more organized and simplified, it only makes sense that you automate your payments. You can also automate your savings, debt payments, and bills. The easier you can make your life under your new budget, the better.

Chapter 2:
Shifting Your Mindset from Unnecessary Spending and Debt Build-Up to Simple and Smart Spending & Budgeting

2.1

Minimalism isn't discussed much in terms of its philosophies. It tends to be more talked about methodologically. In order to have a minimalist budget, it's important to get into a minimalist mindset. This is a mindset of someone who makes it a choice to live a minimal life and make it the root of their behavior.

This isn't just some mindless fad. How can it be when it requires a bit of sacrifice and some limitations? Generally, most people who make the decision to simplify their life do this because they start to think differently about how they can live their best life, or they notice the destructive and immoral nature of thoughtless consumerism and make that conscious effort to get rid of their own demons.

If you don't cultivate the right mindset, your budget is going to be a constant battle. You will try to resist those temptations. You will try to reduce mental and physical clutter. You will try to find solutions. But during all of this, your inner urges will grow. A lot like an extreme diet, minimalism without the right mindset will leave you destined to relapse. When you have to push against your own desires, it becomes a losing battle.

So if you're not supposed to fight against your own desires, what are you supposed to do? This isn't meant to tell you to give up on trying to live a simpler life. I want to make sure that you are realistic about this so that you can make your life easier. The right mindset for a minimalist budget isn't about fighting your desires; it's about learning how to not desire.

Once you have cultivated the right mindset, you will find that you are no longer fighting a losing battle. You will be driven by your motives, and your actions will fall into place. You will love the simplicity, and you will understand the reasons behind these actions.

This mindset is best seen as a reduction based on priorities. It doesn't mean that you have to get rid of and stop buying things that you enjoy and wish that you could have all of them back. It means that you will make reductions at a decent pace, and over time you will start to represent the things that are really important.

Objects and things are the most commonly pictured cut back, but when it comes to a minimalist mindset, it also applies to activities and relationships—including with yourself, speech, and all aspects of your life. You will learn to make reductions based on priorities. This will make room for the things that really matter to you.

2.2

Most people don't understand why you want to live a life within a minimalist budget. They don't understand why you aren't taking advantage of all the luxuries and invention that are available.

They believe they have earned the right to live however they want and by any means necessary. This is true. What they don't understand is that living a life with a minimalist budget will benefit you in ways that they don't understand.

1. **Decluttering will help you breathe.**

   When you start reducing the things you buy and start getting rid of things in your home, it will open up more space in your life. You find that you have more room to move around. More importantly, you will no longer be holding onto things that aren't giving you anything. You'll find new freedom in less stuff cluttering your life, and this includes those credit card bills. All of this means you will be able to breathe easier.

2. **Minimalism will give you the chance to refocus.**

   When you have a lot of stuff, your focus will be everywhere. You are constantly worried about making enough money to pay for everything, and you spend your time looking for places to put away everything. When all of this stuff is gone and your bills are lessened, it will become possible for you to focus your energy and time on things that are important, like the things and people around you.

3. **Buying less means more money.**

   When you start cutting back on things, other things will open up. The money that you will have spent buying things you don't need, maintaining things, and making sure you have the latest stuff, will be in your pocket and not in a store. You will be able to pay off your debts, and you will eventually free up even more money. You will depend on money a lot less.

4. **You will have more time.**

   When you require less money to live, you won't have to work as much. This will give you more time. You also won't have to spend as much time dealing with those extra things. You will be able to focus on your time so that you can do the things you enjoy.

5. **You will have more energy.**

   When you don't have all the clutter, the energy you will have spent dealing with all of this will become available for other things. People who don't have to deal with a materialistic life are stronger and healthier as a result.

It can seem daunting to develop the right mindset for a minimalist budget, but with the right steps, you will be there in no time.

1. **Start Small**

   If you are like the majority of Americans drowning in the debt of the American Dream, take a look at your bills and stuff, and wonder if you can even find freedom in all of this. The first thing you need to do is to focus on one small area that you can purge. This can be as simple as your purse or wallet. This is just one step that is manageable and will set you up for success in the long run.

   Instead of thinking that you must do everything in one fell swoop, do things in little chunks. Budget your time each day to accomplish something that will get you closer to your minimalist budget. Your hard work is going to build up, and you will be amazed at how little effort it will take.

2. **Assign Value**

   If you want to have a successful minimalist budget, you have to learn how to figure out the value of things. Creating this budget will involve fixing up your house as well as your bank account. When you go through your house and clean out things, you may find yourself faced with the question, "what if I need it later?"

   Having a minimalist mindset means you will have to figure out what are the things that are essential, and you can't do that without understanding your ultimate purpose. If you aren't going to find meaning and success in the things that you have, where will you look? How are you going to design your life to find them? It will probably take some mind retraining to place value on things that you can't actually touch. Maybe instead of purchasing stuff, you decide you want to pursue outdoor adventures, physical fitness, or generosity. Whatever it is that gives your life purpose, keep it your focus and center yourself on that.

3. **Watch Out for Sentimentality**

Gifts from birthdays and holidays, especially kid's gifts, can easily pile up for anybody. No matter what causes the pileup, a lot of people will have trouble managing these things. A lot of people will feel guilty about getting rid of these things, especially those gifts that you are meant to figure out what to do with. Family heirlooms have the same kind of weight. It depends on whether they hold any real value.

Try taking photos of things that you are sentimental about. This will give you something to remember it by without it taking up your time and money to maintain.

4. **Stop Comparing**

This is the hard-learned truth when it comes to living within your means. Yes, you need to quit making a comparison. Most people think that they have to have something to measure up to somebody else. Instead of looking at what other people are doing, try looking at yourself. Get rid of Facebook for 30 days, avoid going to the malls, and stop reading luxurious magazines. Find out what you need. You will probably find that it isn't much stuff.

5. **Check Your Cart**

With online shopping, it is extremely easy to accumulate a lot of stuff you don't need and waste money. Instead of checking out as soon as you have found the things you *need*, leave those items in your cart for a few days or weeks even. In the majority of the time, you will discover that you have forgotten about them never really needed them, to begin with. This works anytime that there is a chance for an impulse buy.

6. **Remove the Value of Your Purchases**

Everything that we buy will hold some sort of value for our lives. That means it's up to use to figure out what is actually necessary versus what is superfluous when we are buying things. For example, you may be buying food because you actually need to eat or because you are just bored and want to eat. You may go clothes shopping and buy things that you want because they are trendy, or you may buy clothes that you actually need. You may buy a glass of wine because you actually want one, or you may get one just because everybody else around you is having a glass, and you don't want to feel left out.

The important thing is to remember these wise words, "you can't have everything you want, but you can love everything you have." View life as if you were traveling full-time on a budget. It will change the way you buy services and goods. You will have to justify the costs to support your lifestyle. You will be less likely to buy all of those souvenirs and little knick-knacks that you like but won't be useful for you. Everything you buy will likely have many different uses. For example, clothing items will probably match with the majority of your wardrobe, charging cables must work on multiple devices, and how much you spend on certain items will depend on how useful and how long you plan on using them.

When you purchase things with a critical eye, it will help you evaluate how much value, or lack thereof, a purchase will contribute to the quality of your life. Thinking twice about the things that you spend your money on and discovering ways to extract value from the things you buy will make sure that your purchases will end up being deliberate, being put to good use, and being worth the money you spend on them.

Your Quick Start Action Step:

If you're trying to really supercharge that minimalist mindset right now, here are a few tips.

1. **Get Inspired**

   Go online and look at minimalist spaces, or you can read some blogs or magazines that focus on this type of thing.

2. **Have More Experience**

   Millennials sort of already have this down. They are interested in having experiences instead of having stuff. Try spending any extra income you have on doing things instead of getting things,s and see if this makes you feel better.

3. **Find Encouragement in Community**

   Chances are that the struggles you have faced and will face as you transition to a minimalist budget lifestyle isn't anything new. Somebody else has probably gone through this before. Reach out to those people for help and inspiration.

4. **Practice!**

   This is a journey that will never stop. You have to work on it little by little. Start saying no to more and more things, and it will become easier. The same goes for getting rid of things. Become aware of how this will make you even happier. Don't get upset if you notice that these things feel like a challenge.

Chapter 3: Reviewing Your Personal Finances

3.1

Having a budget may sound like an unrealistic and simplistic way to manage your income. There are some people who may think that it is ineffective in the grand scheme. The fact of the matter is, budgets don't work unless you make them work. You can handle this by sitting down, coming up with it, and then reviewing it on a regular basis.

You won't know the effectiveness of it until you have given it a try. If you are currently struggling to make ends meet, balance what you make with what you spend then save money. This will be a lot easier if you allocate your budget.

This doesn't mean that you just make it, but you also have to actively use it. Your budget can range from simple to complex. There are loads of software available that can help you come up with your budget that works with your personal needs and lifestyle. You can even use a blank word document or a piece of paper.

After you have come up with your budget, the next important thing that you have to do is to review it on a regular basis. If it's not reviewed regularly, you won't know if it is still working for you. Budgets are ongoing, changing, and working documents that will change along with your life.

3.2

You have to remember that keeping a budget and reviewing it regularly isn't about deprivation. It's about making sure you stay proactive in the way that you use your money. You need to find creative ways to get the most out of it while you stick to the plan that is designed to give you a chance to live well and save adequately while living with peace of mind and surplus.

If you are brand new to your budgeting process, you will find that the first few months are going to be about coming up with your goals and setting them as realistically as you can. If you intend on meeting all of your goals, you will likely have to make a few adjustments. The longer you maintain your budget, the less frequent these adjustments will become.

Another important thing about your monthly review is that if you are married, make sure you do these reviews together. It's fine if one of you wants to take the lead in getting the numbers together, but you both share in the decision-making process and, likely, the money-making process. Oftentimes, financial disagreements are caused by assumptions about who spent what. Looking at the numbers every month will do wonders for clarity and will foster teamwork and communication.

3.3

Understanding your budget and where your money is going is crucial for a minimalist budget. Make sure that you follow these steps to stay in control of your finances. Everything you do in this section and in the action steps will be helpful when you reach chapter seven and create your actual budget.

1. **Review Your Spending**

   You need to make sure that you understand how you spend your money. This is the most important part of a review. This is going to help you work out where you are able to save some money.

   Take a look at your bank statements. This can help you find most things that you have to spend money on using your credit or debit card. You will also be able to find the amount of cash that you take out every week.

In the future, it will be a good idea to make a record of your spending. This is going to give you a better idea of where all of your money is being spent and how you can save some.

2. Identify Areas for Possible Savings

You may be able to reduce your bills for things such as your cell phone and electricity and not have to sacrifice on quality. You must also look at some of the most common ways that people tend to throw away money. And if you are going to college, you can check to see if you are paying for things that you can also be getting for free.

3. Find Help if You Need It

At this point, you must have a pretty good understanding of what your financial situation looks like, but if things are pretty serious, you may need to find some help.

If you are currently a student, with a little bit of research, you can find an emergency grant or loan. If you are majorly in debt, you can get some free advice from debt counselors on what you must do.

You may even find yourself considering a payday loan to help you make ends meet. These tend to be extremely expensive and will likely just make your bad situation even worse, so make sure that you look carefully at your alternatives.

4. Have You Looked at All of Your Expenses?

This may sound like a dumb question, but more often than not, this is the main thing that will get people in trouble when it comes to accounts and budgeting.

Sure, everybody is aware of their typical expenses, such as gas, electric, water, mortgage, and so on. But it's also important that you look at those once a month or year expenses that don't necessarily have a due date but must be put into your budget, lest they are forgotten.

Some of these types of things may include medication, dog food, toiletries, yearly subscriptions to things like Amazon Prime and car registration. These types of things can end up running out at very random times, but it is absolutely necessary to purchase if you were to run out of toilet paper.

Since most of these aren't recurring expenses with a set due date, they are often easily needed when you aren't expecting them. And if all of your money has been set aside for the week on other needed items, these needs can easily catch you by surprise, and you will end up being unprepared. If you end up being unprepared, then your credit card will end up taking a hit.

The best thing for you to do is to sit down with your family and hash out all of the small expenses that may end up coming up during the year. Create a chart that has every month on it, and then write out all of these little expenses that may come up during the month. You can't leave anything out. These expenses may be school supplies (especially in the month of August) new clothes, or money to set aside for Halloween candy.

Then, for every succeeding month of doing your budget, have this list ready so that you are able to account for each of these small expenses that will come up during the next month. It may even help if you break these expenses down by week. If you want to do this, all you need to do is add the expense to a specific line instead of just the month.

For example, let's assume that you are going to need $100 to get some new clothes for your children before school starts back. Decide on the week that you are going to go shopping and then place that purchase on that week's total. This will help you to make sure that you are prepared and that you will have plenty of money to get your job done, without ending up over budget.

If, after your first meeting, you or a family member discovers that there is another expense coming up in the next few months that you haven't accounted for, then add it into your list so that you are prepared.

You have to remember that there isn't an expense that is too small to worry about. If you make sure to think about it now, then there is a good chance that you won't be caught off guard when you are faced with the expense.

5. **Are All of the Numbers Firm, or Can You Change Them?**

This is a pretty hard question to answer, but it is a pretty relevant one. You have to know if any of the expenses that you have during the month are able to be changed—and if they are, will you be able to still make the payment?

For example, let's say that you just moved into a new house and are running your AC quite a bit. You average around $110 each month for your electric utilities, which works perfectly into your budget, so all is well.

However, the weather quickly gets colder. When this change happens, it causes a change in your electric bill, sending it all the way up to $150. This is a little bit higher than you have been used to, but you can still handle it with just a few little tweaks to your budget.

Then, say the next month, your bill jumps up to $229. The following month, you get a bill of $272. That puts you at over $160 than what you have been originally paying. To say the least, you will be quite shocked. Now, this is a new house, as we've stated earlier, so you will be better prepared the next year. But that still means you are going to have to do some strategic planning to get those bills paid now.

So how can you prevent this surprise? Go through all of your bills, and find those that can all of a sudden change on you. Most of your bills will probably have a flat rate, like $21 for trash pickup or $20 for internet, but there are some that are based on your usage of their service. The usual ones are cell phone service, water utilities, and electric utilities.

After you have figured out when bills can end up fluctuating, keep tabs on when they are more likely to change. With our example above, it will be a safe bet that the electric bill is going to go up quite a bit during the winter, so that means you will need to be more progressive with your budget from November to February so that you don't end up getting caught off guard when you get the bill.

Alongside this, you will also want to know where you are able to pull extra funds from just in case you do end up getting caught off guard. It's important that you always have a fallback if there is a time that a bill may trip you up. When you have a plan, you will be able to prevent late payments and charges, and you will be less likely to have to turn to your credit card to compensate for the difference.

6. **Do You Have Enough Spending Money for Unexpected Expenses?**

This can be a big problem for people, especially if they have large amounts of credit card debt. There are a lot of people that will try to pay off their cards each month without incurring any interest, which means that they are going to have to sacrifice their spending money to hit what they need to each month. But when they do this, they are forcing themselves to have to use the credit card to make their monthly payments, which means that they are going to be stuck in a never-ending cycle.

It is extremely important that you leave yourself plenty of spending money. If you are having to pay off debt, it can be extremely attractive to throw every penny you have to it. However, take this piece of advice: you will be paying off those credit cards for a lot longer if you don't allow yourself extra money first and then pay on the debt.

Make sure that every week, you give yourself some spending money. This can be left in your bank, and you can spend it from there. However, it is often better if you pull out the cash. Cash is very visual—so with just a glance, you will know exactly how much you have to spend, and you won't be able to overspend your cash like you can with a card.

The amount that you choose to keep on you for spending will depend on your family and your budget. Find what works best for you, and don't sacrifice. It's better to be prepared than to have to turn to credit when something unexpected comes up.

Your Quick Start Action Step:

The following are some quick action steps that you can make to get your finances under control.

1. **Check Your Bank Balance**

   This is the quickest and easiest thing you can do to take control of your money, and this can be one of the scariest things to know. You have to understand where your situation is, which means that you need to know the amount of money you have or the amount that you owe.

- Sign into your online bank account, and find out how much money you have left or how overdrawn you are.

- You will then need to look at other debts you may owe. This may mean credit cards or loans that you haven't paid off yet. You must not consider student loans because they work differently.

- Lastly, look at your savings to see what you have. It is best to leave these funds alone—but if you are in a lot of debt, you may want to use some of this to pay off them off because it can help you save more money in the long run. This is why it's important to know what you have.

2. **Check Your Income**

Understanding the amount of money that you earn in each month is important to understand your finances. The income you get each month can come from the money from your family, benefits, pay from work, scholarships, bursaries, and student loans.

You will probably receive money from different places at different times during the month. For example, your job may pay you every week or once a month, but your student loan will come in at the beginning of the term. To fully understand the amount you have to spend, try to work out the monthly or weekly equivalent for each of your income types. This is going to help you avoid spending your entire loan within the first few weeks of the term or spending out too much during the holidays when you work more instead of saving it for when you go back to school or when your hours get cut.

Chapter 4:
Simplified Financial Planning Goes a Long Way

4.1

Financial planning is ongoing, and it's there to help you make sensible decisions about your money so that you can achieve your life goals. This planning process may involve creating wills to help protect your family, thinking about how the family will live if you aren't making any income, and what they'll do if you fall ill or die. It is okay to spend your money in different ways, but it also helps when you think about all these things as a whole and when you consider a long-term plan. You can come up with your own plan, or you can hire a financial planner if you really have to. The point of minimalist budgets is to save money, so hiring somebody probably isn't something you must do unless you have a lot of assets.

You can come up with a financial plan in six easy steps:

1. Establish you long- and short-term goals.
2. Write out your liabilities and assets.
3. Check to see how close you are at achieving your goals.
4. Come up with your plan, and create a map to reach your goals.
5. Implement that plan, and make the needed changes.
6. Review and monitor your plan to make adjustments when you need to.

It's important that you work out your life goals and break them down into long- and short-term goals. Once you do this, it's important that you prioritize these things and think about how much it is likely to cost you and when you are going to need the money. This is all to make sure you are ready for anything.

4.2

As boring as it may seem, having a financial plan is crucial for seeing the big picture and setting up all of your goals. These are all important parts of mapping out your financial future. When you have a plan, you will find that it is easier for you to make financial decisions and keep yourself on track to meet those goals.

Now, the point of this book and following a minimalist budget is to be able to do it on your own. There are some people, though, that may already have a certified financial planner that can help them. They *can* help, especially if:

- You have an immediate need or an unexpected life event.

- You don't have the knowledge in certain areas like retirement, investments, taxes, or insurance planning.

- You are looking for a professional opinion about a plan that you came up on your own.

- You don't have the time to do your own planning.

- You are trying to improve how to manage your finances but can't figure out where to start.

Unless you already have one, or you really can't figure out your finances, there is no need to go out and hire a financial planner.

4.3

Through good and bad, thick and thin, those who are successful and coming up with goals and achieving them, at least in finances, are the people who come up with a financial plan and follow through with it. If you are interested in financial security, having a good plan is the way to do it.

The following are eight steps to make sure that you do just that:

1. **Figure Out Where Your Money Goes**

   Once you have taken a look at your finances and figure out where you are like you did in the last chapter, the next thing you have to do is think of where you are going to spend your money now.

   To get started with this, carry around a small notebook that will fit in your pocket or purse. Each time you buy something, write down what it is and how much. At the end of your first week, spend some time going over these notes and categorize them. How much has been spent on food? Transportation? Utilities? Mortgage? Rent? Healthcare? Entertainment? Clothing? Housing? At the end of the first month, consolidate these notes. At the end of the second month, consolidate again.   And then at the three-month mark, add all of your expenses up, and devote a little bit of study time.

   This process is done to get a picture of what you spend money on and not necessarily cutting things out at this point. This will help you have an idea of the things you need and don't need.

2. **Set Your Financial Goals**

   I want you to ask yourself, "Where do I see myself in 20 years?" Stay away from generic things like, "I want to be rich." Give a more specific answer: "I want a house with a mortgage that is almost paid off, and an investment portfolio of $400,000, plus a decent sized savings account for emergency expenses."

   Make sure you are realistic when you set these goals, and try to be specific. Your goal is to succeed, not to fail. This can only be done if you start with attainable and specific goals.

3. Prepare for the Unexpected with Insurance

If you don't have a family, think about getting some disability insurance to protect your earnings. If you do have a family, think about some disability coverage as well as a lot of life insurance to help protect your loved ones. Make sure you have adequate renters or homeowner's insurance, auto coverage, and health insurance. No matter how your finances may look like, making sure that you are prepared for the unexpected will help you stay on track if something comes up.

4. Watch Your Credit Score

It's important to know your credit score. Once a year, check your score with the three biggies. Credit Karma is a great website to get your TransUnion and Experian scores. Make sure that your report doesn't have any discrepancies. Dispute any errors that you may see.

5. Begin Saving

The key to any budget and financial plan is savings, and the money you spend plays a big part in this. Even people with large incomes need to pay attention to what they spend because they can easily spend too much. But if you make sure to control your outgo, it won't matter what your income is because it will always be more than enough.

This is where you use what you have done in the last chapter. You will start cutting back on the things that you don't need from your expenditure. This money that you free up must be put into a savings account. It's a good idea to try to save up three months' worth of income just in case of an emergency. If you do have to use some of this, make sure you replace it.

6. Start to Build a Portfolio

After you have created your emergency fund, you need to look at investing some of your extra cash. For new and experienced investors, one of the easiest things to do is to build a portfolio with mutual funds. You can easily finance mutual funds that match up with your risk tolerance. They also spread your investment risk. Mutual funds will also provide you with professional money management, which is a great idea if you don't have the expertise or time to do this alone.

7. **Keep an Eye on Your Plan**

It's important that you manage your financial plan to make sure that it stays congruent with your situation. Have any of your goals changed? How does your health, family needs, debt, and income look? How are your investments doing? More importantly, have they done what you've expected?

Depending on your circumstances, it may make sense to look over your plan semi-annually or quarterly. If you check your plan multiple times a year, make sure you don't confuse your long-term and short-term goals.

8. **Create an Exit Strategy**

You need an exit strategy that matches with your financial goals. If your plan is to purchase a 10,000-square foot home in ten years, you will need to free some of your portfolios up at that point in order to accomplish that goal. Similarly, if you planned on needing college money for your children, you may want an exit strategy for that as well. You will also need to come up with an exit strategy for yourself when you retire and a plan for your heirs.

9. **Identify and Evaluate Alternative Course of Action**

Coming up with alternatives is important for making the best decisions. There are lots of different factors that will influence your available alternatives; possible courses of action will typically fall into one of these categories:

- Continue your current course of action.
- Expand what your current situation is.
- Change what your current situation is.
- Pick a different course of action.

Not every single one of these categories will be applicable to each of your decision situations. However, they do show you all of your possible courses of action. Having creativity in your decision-making process is crucial in coming up with effective choices. Considering all of your possible alternatives is going to help you make the best and most satisfying decisions.

When you do decide to pick a different course of action, you will need to evaluate the said course. Things you will have to take into consideration are current economic conditions, personal values, and your life situation.

You need to look at the consequences of choices. All of your decisions will close off a different choice. For example, choosing to invest some money in a stock can mean that you aren't able to take a vacation. Choosing to go to school full time may mean that you will not be able to work full time. Opportunity cost is the amount that you will be giving up when you make a choice. This cost, which is often called a trade-off of a decision, won't always be able to be measured in dollars.

Decision making is going to always be a part of your financial and personal situation. Thus, you are going to have to consider the lost opportunities that are going to result from the decisions you make.

Uncertainty is going to be a part of all of your decisions. Choosing a career field and picking a major at college will all involve some sort of risk. What if you discover that you don't like working in that particular field or that you're not able to find any employment?
There are other decisions that involve a lower degree of risk, like putting money into your savings account or buying items that cost just a couple of bucks. The odds of you losing something of great value are very low in these types of situations.

In many different financial decisions, evaluating and identifying risk is pretty hard. The best way for you to consider risk is to get all of the information for it based on your experience and the experiences of other people, and then use financial planning information sources.

Relevant information is needed at every single stage of your decision-making process. Changing economic, social, and personal conditions will require that you are always supplementing and updating your knowledge.

10. Create a Will

Your financial planning doesn't just end when you die. You have to make sure that you make provisions for what is going to happen to your estate once you are gone. At the very least, if you don't have a will written up, your survivors will probably end up in probate court working out some type of deal to distribute all of your assets.

At the worst, the assets may end up disappearing into some black hole. This is the reason why having a properly executed and drawn will is extremely important. This is literally your financial decision with regards to your state of financial affairs.

It's important that you make some time to meet up with your trusted attorney, and then create a will that will be distributed to your estate according to your wishes. You can come up with it now in one way, and then you can make modifications later on when your financial situations change. You may end up being surprised to discover that you are able to find some sort of peace after you have completed your will. That peace comes from the fact that you will know that you have done all that you can in order to take care of your loved ones once you are gone.

Your Quick Start Action Step:

Now, everything we have covered in this chapter can seem a bit daunting, and it may not be clear as to what you can do right now. We're going to look at ten basic steps that you can take now to help you get started.

1. **What are the motives behind your financial choices?**

   Before you come up with your budget and start to make cuts, you need to figure out what you value the most in your life.

2. **Get yourself organized.**

   Make sure that you have all your financial statements in one place where you can easily access them.

3. **Make sure that you know exactly where all of your money goes.**

   I've said this before, and it will probably be mentioned in this book for several times—it is extremely important that you know where your money is going.

4. **Shop in a smarter way.**

   Try to make smart shopping choices to find money without needing to make more.

5. **Look over your debts and reduce them.**

   Figure out all of your debts, and use this book to get them paid off.

6. **Create a stronger credit report.**

   Keeping a strong credit report will help you easily accomplish your financial goals.

7. **Save money for your future life.**

   Make sure that you pay yourself first in order to save up money and to start your strong retirement plan.

8. **Set up your financial goals.**

   Keep track of all of your goals, and celebrate your milestones so that you can reach your dreams faster.

9. **Come up with a spending plan.**

   Use your spending plan to make sure that your daily spending habits don't end up overwhelming your goals.

10. Invest your money in order to reach your goals.

You can watch your money grow by investing some of the extra so that you can reach your longer-term objectives.

Chapter 5:
Unnecessary Compulsive Spending and How to Fix It

5.1

One person's trash is another person's treasure. What may be right for me may not be for you. But I believe that everybody can agree that we all spend money on unnecessary and impractical things that aren't satisfying.

When you don't plan out your big dream, it becomes easy to get distracted by shiny things. Instead of coming up with your life and spending habits to coincide with your real dream, you will continue to work at a place that leaves you with very little free time, and you will spend your money on things you don't need to fill that void. Or you can be interested in buying your own home, but you spend money on things to decorate what you are currently living in to make it feel like the home you want.

Everybody does things that they don't realize until much later. The decision you make right now to get yourself out of debt and saving up money is going to open up doors and spark lots of thoughts that you probably don't have any idea about right now.

5.2

Compulsive spending and shopping can be caused by financial, family, occupational, and interpersonal problems in your life. Some people have such a problem with overspending—and sometimes, it can get to the point of an addiction.

Issues in relationships may happen because of excessive spending, and your efforts to cover up these debts and purchases will only make things worse. People who engage in this kind of shopping may end up becoming pre-occupied with their behavior and can learn how to spend less with some help and time. You may even start to experience anxiety or depression because of your shopping or spending, which can end up affecting your school or work performance.

You may experience financial problems if the money you use is borrowed or if there is excessive use of credit to make your compulsive purchases. Most of the time, the extent of damage you have created only gets discovered once you have accumulated a large sum of debt that will cause the need for a drastic change in your life to fix it.

5.3

If you're tired of compulsive shopping and overspending, then there are several things you can do to overcome this issue.

1. **Do some inventory**

    It's common for people to purchase new stuff just because they can't see the things they already have. Weed out your clothing and get rid of unmatched, ill-fitting, or well-worn ones. This is also true for knickknacks, household products, and tools.

2. **Buy good-quality products**

    This may seem counterintuitive, but it's common for people to never use things that they love and that gives them great pleasure. This is often due to their want to protect it because they love it so much. Instead, they also buy a cheap knockoff to use. Get the good stuff that you love and actually use it, so you don't have to buy a cheaper alternative.

3. **Get rid of temptation**

    Think about having a friend that is constantly telling you about these amazing deals or that you have to try the new pizza place. When you hear these things, it puts you in a place to consider these purchases that you probably won't have thought about.

4. **Wait it out**

When you really want to buy something, think about it for about 20 minutes. After you have let your head clear, reconsider how and when you will actually use it. Instead of deciding whether or not to get it, give yourself a chance to think of something that you may need instead. Typically, these impulse purchases will seem less urgent after you sleep on them.

5. **Remember, it's fine not to buy**

Shopping takes time, and it can end up making you feel like you wasted a lot of time if you don't buy anything. Outlet malls are typically a dangerous place for those who are trying to reduce their consumption. It's common that people will buy things they don't need instead of leaving the store empty-handed so that it doesn't feel like the trip is wasted.

6. **Pay with Cash**

People will normally end up spending a lot more money when they pay with debit cards or credit cards. When you charge items, you will feel more disconnected from your money. You don't see them as dollars.

Spending becomes a lot more real when you have to take the money out of your wallet or purse. This is why it is best that you immediately set money aside from your paycheck for bills, and then take the remaining out in cash. This will make you a lot less likely to go on a compulsive shopping binge because you will have a very limited amount of money to spend.

7. **Fill Up your Life with Social Connections**

   Most of the time, when a person compulsively spends, they are trying to fill their needs by making connections with other people through their shopping. The problem is, they aren't able to ever completely fill in that void.

   That's why it is a good idea to fill up your life with other social activities and connections. These things may include book clubs, charities, sports clubs, and the like.

   Shopping is so often caused by not having as much of a social life—but if instead of shopping, you fill up your days with other things, there will be two things that happen. You will find that you don't wind up at the mall as often, and you will be hanging around with people who don't always go shopping. When you hang around with other shoppers, you will only get more encouragement from them to buy things.

   This is very similar to the rationale behind alcoholics not going to bars. It becomes a lot easier to not make purchases when you aren't being forced to say no to yourself.

Your Quick Start Action Step

The hardest aspect of personal finances is trying to figure out the best way to use your money. It is hard trying to figure out ways to save a lot of money on a tiny budget. The main way to lessen your spending is by cutting back a bit in every area. It may take some work, but you will find your stress begin to go down when you are about to pay off some of your debt. Here are some ways to help you cut back:

- Put all your bonuses into a savings account. It's a great feeling when you change your purse and find a $20 bill. Don't put it in your pocket—rather, pay yourself by putting it into your savings account.

- Cook at home. It's hard to have the time and energy to make a home-cooked meal when you get home from work. Begin cooking twice a week, and slowly increase it one day every week until you are cooking every night. If this isn't realistic for you, take time on the weekend to meal prep some dinners for the week ahead. By doing this, you will have meals ready when you get home. This goes for morning coffee, too. Buying that large specialty coffee each day can add up to a lot of money. Take the time to brew some coffee at home before you leave for work.

- Write down the things you need from the store before you go. If you have ever gone to the store without a list or when hungry, it is tempting to buy more food than normal. Preplan your meals and buy what you need in one trip so that you don't spend money on items you don't need and that you don't forget what you do need. Lists will ensure that you don't have to make another trip to the store and that you aren't faced with temptation.

- Make a shopping limit. Don't buy things on impulse. If you want an expensive coat that you really don't need, wait a few days to see if you are still thinking about it. This lets you check online to find a cheaper alternative.

- Cancel memberships, and cut your entertainment bill. It may be easy to forget about recurring monthly bills. If you have a gym membership that you don't use, it is time to cancel it. If you have a Netflix membership but never use it, cancel it. Getting rid of extra expenses can make a big difference to your budget.

- Learn to love DIY projects. Don't go to a spa to have a facial; make one for yourself. Pinterest has many useful tools for those of you who have the guts to try it. You can find recipes, cleaning hacks, and ways to use things around your house.

- Use an app to help you budget. It is easy to overspend when you don't set limits for yourself. Apps like Quicken and Mint can help you track monthly, weekly, and daily spending so that you can see where you must cut back and so that you can get advice for your financial goals and needs.

Chapter 6:
Dealing with Debt

6.1

The simplest way to describe debt is money that is owed from one party to the other. It may get complicated quickly. It all depends on the amount of debt you have and the way you handle it. Debt can be a useful tool or baggage that complicates your life.

Knowing the right way to handle debt can be difficult especially if you constantly struggle to cover your monthly bills. There are various ways to handle each type of debt. There are also ways to get relief from debt. Just be careful of companies that sound too good to be true or promise you absurd things. Here are the two most common types of debt and ways to handle them:

- **Secured debt**: A secured debt is one where the borrower has provided some asset as collateral to secure the loan. Mortgages and car loans are examples of a secured debt. If you don't pay, the creditor can take the said asset like foreclosing your house or repossessing your car.

- **Unsecured debt** is never backed by an asset. One example is a credit card. This doesn't mean you won't have consequences if you don't pay your bills. The creditor can sell your debt to a collection agency that will then call you night and day for payment. If you still don't pay, they might be able to sue you for payment. This might lead to your wages being garnished. Some creditors might sue you without using a collection agency.

6.2

Most people wonder how much of their money is theirs and the amount they pay toward debt factors in on how their debt is accumulated. There are many reasons why we have debt, such as unemployment or unforeseen emergencies. More often than not, debt is caused by bad spending habits. If you aren't paying with cash, it will cost you to spend money.

Think about a credit card being somebody who is granting you a favor to buy things you cannot afford but will let you pay them off later. Actually, the truth is you just wind up owing more and not getting everything you need.

Everybody alive tries to keep up with their neighbors. They have the life we've always wished for, and we will never be able to keep up with them. These things we long for lead us to huge amounts of debt. When we don't know how to manage this debt, it can cause our credit card bills to grow endlessly.

Let's look at making a purchase of $500 without a credit card. You think this is a good deal because you only have to pay $15 a month. This is very manageable for you. What you don't realize is the creditor is adding an additional $147 to that bill for interest. If you only pay $15 each month, it is going to take you four years to pay off that $500 charge. That is assuming you have an interest rate of 14.7 percent. If your credit card has a higher interest rate, this purchase at 22 percent means you are going to be paying out an additional $280 in interest. Yes, you still have those four years to pay off a total of $780, so is that item worth that much more?

If you add in all our wants with the large investments of cars and homes along with the planned necessities like weddings and college as well as the unplanned emergencies like relocation, unemployment, and medical emergencies, it is easy to visualize how quickly debt can grow. The main reason people get into debt is a combination of personal and impersonal finances.

6.3

Even if your debt is small, you have to manage it well. You have to make your payments on time and be sure it doesn't get out of hand. If your debt is large, you must put in more effort to pay it off while making your other payments.

1. **Know your creditors and the amounts you owe.**

    Create a list of debts that include the creditor, complete amount you owe, how much your payments are, and when they are due. Use a credit report to confirm your debts. Having the debts in front of you lets you see the bigger picture, so you are aware of your whole debt. Don't make a list and then forget about it. Look at it from time to time, especially when you pay your bills. Update the list every month or two when the list changes.

2. **Pay your dues on time.**

    Making late payments will make it harder for you to pay off the debt because you are going to have to pay an extra late fee for each payment you miss. If you miss two payments, your finance charges and interest rate will go up. If you use a calendar, place your payments and set an alarm to give you an alert a couple days before the payment needs to be made. If you miss a payment, don't wait until it becomes due again. The creditor may report it to a credit bureau. Make your payment once you remember.

3. **Make a bill-paying calendar.**

    Use a calendar to help you figure out what bill to pay with a certain paycheck. Write every bill's payment on the day it is due. Next, put in the calendar when you get paid. If you get paid on the same date, this is an easy step for you. If your paychecks come on a different day, it will help to make a note each month.

4. **Always make your minimum payment.**

If the minimum amount is all you can pay, that is fine—just do it on time. This isn't going to get you any progress in paying off your debt. It will keep the debt from growing and will keep your account good. If you miss a payment, it becomes harder to get caught up. Your account may go into default.

5. **Figure out what debt you need to pay off fastest.**

    Paying off any credit card debt first is the best strategy since these have higher interest rates. It must be the priority since it will cost you the most money. Use your list of debts, and rank them in order that you want to pay them off. You may also choose to pay off the one with the lowest balance first.

6. **Pay off any charge-offs and collections.**

    You can only pay what you can afford. If you have limited funds to repay debts, try to focus on keeping other accounts in good standing. Never sacrifice good accounts for ones that have already changed your credit. Pay the past due accounts when you can afford them. These creditors are going to keep hounding you for payment until it is brought current.

7. **Have an emergency fund to help out in hard situations.**

    You may have to go into debt to cover an emergency if you don't want to dip into your savings account. A small emergency fund can cover small expenses that may pop up now and then. Begin by working to create a small fund. An amount of $ 1,000 is a great place to start. When you have that amount, try to increase it to another thousand. You want to try to create a reserve that equals your six months' pay.

8. **Create a monthly budget to plan expenses.**

Keeping a budget will help you make sure that you have the money to cover all expenses each month. Plan in advance so that you can take action if you are going to be short one month. Budgets help you plan how to use any extra money you may have left after all expenses have been paid. You may have enough money to pay another debt off.

9. **See the signs that you are in need of help.**

If you see that it is too hard for you to pay your bills and debts every month, you can turn to a debt relief company for help. Check out credit counseling agencies in your area. Other options are bankruptcy, debt settlement, and debt consolidation. All of these have disadvantages and advantages, so check each option carefully. If you have a spending problem, you can seek help through a Debtors Anonymous group. This is similar to Alcoholics Anonymous.

10. **Change Your Debt Like Behaviors**

In order to get out of debt, you have to eliminate the reasons you may up in debt in the first place. Even winning the PowerBall Jackpot won't fix your problem if you don't learn how to spend less than what you make.

Everybody has their own reasons for winding up in debt. Medical bills, job loss, school, or just plain young stupidity are all widely common reasons. However, the reason you have gotten into debt doesn't matter all that much. What matters the most is that you don't let this happen again. Here are some things you must not do:

- If you have to take out $50k in student loans to get your bachelor's degree, don't take out an extra $100k for a Ph.D.

- Did you end up falling into a large pile of debt when you lost your job? Resolve, after you have gotten out of debt, to work on building up an emergency fund so that you won't have to face this problem again.

- If you spend several years living a life that you can't afford, then you have to figure out the life that you can actually afford, and get to that point.

That last point is a lot easier said than done. The truth is that the last point is the main reason for this book and about a third of all financial articles you can find online. Let's be honest: how many articles have you seen that are labeled, "Live within your means," "Spend less than your monthly income," and so on? Why has there been so much stuff written on this very simple concept?

This is because after a person has gotten used to living in a certain way, it is extremely hard to change that habit. It will be like having to live on ramen after living for two years on The Capital Grille.

11. When to Refinance or Consolidate

Two of the most common things people do when faced with a lot of debt is consolidation and refinancing. Consolidation means that you put all of your debts into one loan. This will help you by allowing you to deal with only one lender. This means you won't be faced with several different monthly billing statements.

Refinancing means that you replace all of your old debts with a new loan. The goal of doing this is to get a lower interest rate. The majority of students will use consolidation for their student loans. This works if all of the debts are from a government program.

There are many different online calculators to help you figure out if refinancing works for you and to make sure that you pick the best one. Before you decide to consolidate or refinance, take the following into consideration:

- Has your credit score gone up any? This will place you in a favorable light with lenders. This means you will be able to start a tangible process of removing all of your old debt with a new lender that offer better terms.

- Do you already have low-interest rates? If this is the case, you can take advantage of it. Change your variable rate to a fixed rate.

- Are you able to change your payment terms? Dragging your debt along with you for a long time won't help you to become debt-free. If you are making more money and can afford it, start making larger payments each month.

Your Quick Start Action Step:

You are not alone in your debt. Most people in the world are also in debt. If you live in denial, it will only increase your money problems along with your anxiety. When you can face your situation, paying off those debts may be easier than you realize.

- Fast facts: The first thing you have to do is to figure out how big your problem is. Start by looking at your last bank statement and finding any missing paperwork. Open bills you have been neglecting. Create a list of the amount you owe every company and their interest rates. When you have figured out this information, you will begin to prioritize all your debts.

- Transfer to a zero-percent credit card. If you have expensive credit cards, see if you can transfer the debt to a zero-percent credit card. These cards can eliminate interest charges for a certain period. This makes sure that every cent you repay will go toward paying down your balance. In order to get the most out of these cards, you need to pay off the balance in the offer window. If you know you can't repay the whole amount in the introductory period, look for low-interest rate cards. You are still going to pay interest every month, but it will be at a low rate. These types of cards require an unblemished credit score.

- Think about overdraft options. If you pay a lot of interest in overdraft fees, this can quickly accelerate your debt problems. If you think you may be paying too much for your overdraft service, see if your bank has a different account you can switch to, or drop the overdraft from your account entirely.

- You may consider a personal loan. There may be a time when getting a personal loan can help you manage your debt. Find a leading market rate with the APR lower than what you are currently paying on your credit card. If you look around, it may be possible to find a rate lower than eight percent. This is a lot better than the normal 17 to 22 percent that normal credit cards charge. If you need to borrow a large sum of money, a personal loan is a way to go. Larger loans usually come with lower APRs than those with smaller amounts. Don't borrow more money than you need since this may increase your chances of getting deeper into debt. Always shop around. You aren't going to get a good rate if you accept the first offer from the first lender you go to.

Chapter 7: Overall Budget Techniques Applied to Daily, Monthly, and Long-Term Expenses

7.1

We've used the word budget and budgeting a lot throughout this book. While it may sound like a bad word to many, especially for those who know how taking a deeper look at their finances is going to reveal some pretty bad habits that they would rather stay hidden, it is an extremely helpful tool when it comes to a minimalist budget.

Budgeting is known to be difficult, even when it comes to just keeping track of where all of your money goes. The first question people will ask you is if you are trying to budget before taxes (i.e. gross income) or after taxes (i.e. net income)?

If you want to begin with your gross income, it will be best to look at the percentage that is saved in your 401(k). If your company offers you a match offer, make sure you put away enough to get it. The maximum contribution of an employee for a 401(k) is $18,000 in 2016, so try not to go over this limit. However, this does not include what your employer will contribute. The limit for you and your employer's contribution is $53,000. You can also have health insurance premiums that are automatically deducted from your pay if your company provides you insurance, so there is a chance that you won't have to include this into your post-tax budget.

After you have become comfortable with how your payroll and pre-tax deduction saving works, you can then focus on your budget for net income, which is what most people look at day-to-day. If you plan on being really minimalist with your budget, here is a suggestion: the 65-25-10 rule.

- 65% is spent on your day-to-day living.
- 25% is spent on large expenses and retirement, including emergencies.
- 10% is given away to your favorite causes or charity.

You can get really nitty-gritty about it, and break them down even further. However, when you are trying to see the big picture, sometimes it's good just to have a few numbers. If you have to provide your own savings, then you may want the breakdown to be 65-15-10-10.

- 65% is still day-to-day expenses.
- 15% is your emergency and large expenses.
- 10% is retirement expenses.
- 10% is charity expenses.

The hard decisions are made in the day-to-day expenses. If you make sure that you automate your savings money and set them aside, you will make sure that you won't spend the amount that you intended to save on eating out or impulse buys because the money won't be in your checking account.

When you are first starting out with budgeting, or when you are trying to get a handle on your spending, try using a cash-only method or limit yourself a lot when it comes to using your credit card. If you do use a credit card, start going in and manually categorizing and entering your purchases so that you will become aware of the things you are spending.

Much like how you log your calories when you want to lose weight, typing in each dollar you spend into a spreadsheet will help you to become more aware of the way you use your money, which is the first step you need to take toward financial success.

After you have gotten a handle on your spending, you can upgrade to a program that will download your credit card and bank information so that you won't have to write everything down by hand, but make sure that you still set aside some time to really look over your weekly spending so that you can see how you are balancing yourself across different categories. If you overspend in one category, that's okay—just try to under-spend in another one.

This budgeting will require a bit of work on your part—but in the end, it will help you save for and spend on the things that are the most important.

7.2

Even though it is extremely important and significant, financial education isn't something that is normally taught in our educational system. The skills to budget and the ability to stick to a said budget are elusive skills to most. However, it is crucial that you develop these skills because it guarantees your material survival.

Since there is a lack of financial knowledge in the consumer society, there are two major problems that must be faced:

1. Downsizing but not sacrificing on the fun things; and
2. Controlling finances while coming up with a budget.

Based on minimalism principles, it helps to outline some basic rules while providing you with many different ways to curb frivolous spending and to save money. When you figure out what you need, you will be able to live a lifestyle that is more manageable.

Everybody can benefit from living a simpler life. Minimalism not only helps your mental and physical health, but it is also able to improve your financial health. There are several straightforward methods to help you keep your finances on track:

- Improve spending habits – Start incorporating a minimalist approach to your finances, and stay away from becoming a compulsive consumerist. You control your spending habits through learning the psychological traps that end up causing overspending.

- Feel financially secure – You learn budgeting methods, such as fixed-amount budgeting, ratio-based, and A-Z. Make use of a budgeting software program, and create a solid savings strategy to help get you out of debt and get yourself ready for retirement.

- Stop hating your finances. Improve your self-confidence with budgeting tips and learn *smart* financial goals.

Your financial health directly indicates your overall health. That means that it is crucial to truly evaluate your finances and improve your relationship with money. As scary as this may seem, downsizing can positively affect your wellbeing, financially and physically. Minimalism will teach you that you don't actually need as much as you believe you do. Less really is more. Instead of constantly shuffling to keep up with a lifestyle of spending, spend less and then only spend on the things that you really need. Save up your money so that you can invest in your future.

Money management is an important skill for everybody that consumes or earns. Regardless of how large your income is, you can still budget, increase your self-worth, and save money.

Once you have learned how to budget your money, you will be able to clearly see the areas where your money is going, when you get it, and where you can save. This will not only help you reduce your debts, but you will then have bigger savings for those larger expenses, such as a vacation or a car. This means that budgeting is a lifestyle change, and a minimalist budget can completely change your life.

Reading this book is going to be a lot different from actually applying the things that you have learned. You can take notes and mark pages, but once you put this down, you can end up forgetting everything you're supposed to do. That's where the how and action steps come into play.

7.3

Having a budget means more than just getting your bills paid on time. Having a budget involves figuring out how much you must spend and on what. The 50/20/30 budget provides you with a proportional guide to keep your spending aligned with your savings goals.

Adults, especially those that are just starting out, are able to benefit by following along with this simple principle. Once you know the best way to achieve a balanced budget, you are then able to take the next steps to further customize the budget around your own needs.

This 50/20/30 rule is able to help those twenty-somethings begin to sort out the complicated world of finances. It's important that you make an effort to get yourself into a habit—and when you do that, budgeting will become a lot easier in your life. Sure, you are able to make a few tweaks here and there, but try to stay close to the core of this concept. This way, you are guaranteed to gain financial ground instead of losing it.

Before you do anything else, you need to figure out your monthly net income. This is the amount of money that you bring home at the end of each month. There are a lot of people that have deductions taken from their check, which includes medical insurance, HSA funding, and retirement contributions. You can base your budget on the money you actually receive, or you can add these things back in. Either way is going to work, but I think you will get a better picture if you add these numbers back in.

Let's say that after deductions, you bring home $4,000 a month. The deductions are currently $800 for insurances, $100 for HAS, and $600 for 401(k). Adding those back in, your true take-home will be $5,500.

You will place this amount at the top of your spreadsheet, and this is what you base your budget on.

50% of your income must go to essentials.

To start following this rule, set aside half of your income, and no more, for the absolute necessities for living. This may sound like a pretty large percentage, but when you start to consider everything that belongs in this category, it will make more sense.

So that you are completely clear, essential expenses are the things that you will almost certainly have to pay—no matter where you live, where you work, or what your future plans are. In general, these types of expenses are pretty much the same for everybody and will include utility bills, transportation costs, food expenses, and rent/housing amortization. This percentage amount will allow you to adjust it while also maintaining a balanced and sound budget. Keep in mind that this is more about the total sum than it is about each individual cost. For instance, there are some that live in high-rent areas, but they can walk to work; others have cheaper housing, but the transportation is more expensive.

Figuring out how much you absolutely need to live each month is critical to creating your budget. It is best if you look at your last few months of spending to make sure that you get an accurate picture. Make sure that you don't estimate. Trust me—you will not get it right. Everybody pretty much will underestimate the amount of money they spend. For example, most people will not want to admit how much they actually spend on dining out.

Remember: this section includes everything you need to have in order to keep your life going.

The hardest part here is to separate the wants from the needs. You may be needing some new clothes, but that doesn't mean you need to buy them from Niemen Marcus.

Some people need to have an internet connection at home for school or work, but there are some people for whom it is a luxury.

It is important that you are honest with yourself with what you truly need and the things that you don't.

With the income example from above, 50% of your income will be $2,750. Let's say then that you have a fixed expense and items with a set payment that may look like this:

- $100 credit card payment
- $250 car payment
- $350 utility payment
- $600 insurance payment
- $800 rent payment

Then, you have your semi-discretionary items, which are items that will vary each month:

- $25 for basic clothing
- $225 for gas
- $400 for groceries

Depending on your lifestyle, you may also have expenses such as child-related expenses, as well as home or vehicle maintenance.

Your total needs then come out to be $2,750. Depending on your actual situation, you may find that you will have to allocate more of your budget to your essentials. This is okay especially when you are just getting your finances under control. Plus, these numbers are perfect world numbers. There aren't going to be too many people who will have these types of numbers.

The point of this is you have to work on your budget until you are actually about to make these percentages work. You will probably have to pay off debt when you first start. Once that's taken care of, you will have more money to use elsewhere.

20% of your income must go to savings.

The next thing you need to do is to dedicate 20 percent of your take-home pay to savings. This must include rainy-day funds, debt payments, and savings plans. These are things that need to be added but will not endanger your living or cause you to end up homeless if you don't. That may seem like an oversimplification, but hopefully, you understand what I mean. You must only pay this category once you have taken care of your essentials and before you even start thinking about your personal spending.

This must be viewed as your "get ahead" category. The portion of 50% or less is the goal for your essentials, while 20% or more needs to be the goal of this section. This will mean that you can pay off debt quicker, and you will make more significant strides toward a stress-free future by devoting as much of your money as you safely can to this area.

The word retirement probably doesn't seem that important at the age of 24, but it will become even more pressing in the decades to come. Keep in mind that there is a large advantage in starting early especially when it comes to compounded interests and letting your funds grow.

With the previous example, you have $1,100 for this category. Depending on your actual situation, here are a few recommendations for this:

- If you are in debt and working to pay it off, I recommend creating an emergency fund of $1,000, and then use the remaining money to pay off your debt.

- After you have gotten yourself out of debt, I recommend coming up with a larger emergency fund, which will be worth three to six months of essential expenses.

- After your debt has been paid off and you have created your emergency fund, your full 20% can go into savings—and it will be the best feeling in the world.

Saving up your money is one of the most important things you can do for financial success. After you have learned how to delay the gratification and after you are able to place yourself first in your spending equations, you will find that it is easier to get ahead.

30% of your income goes to personal expenses.

This is the last category and the one that will make the biggest difference when it comes to your budget. These are unnecessary expenses that enhance your life. There are a lot of financial experts that see this as completely discretionary, but modern society has caused many of these luxuries to become more mandatory. This will all depend on the things that you want in life and the things that you are willing to sacrifice on. The main reason why this section is larger than the savings section is that there are a lot of things that go in it.

These expenses include things like coffee shop trips, cable bill, and cell phone plan. If you work on-the-go or travel a lot for work, a cell phone plan will become more of a necessity instead of a luxury. However, there is a bit of wiggle room since you can choose your service tier. Other things that fall into this category are dining out, weekend trips, and gym memberships. Only you are able to choose which expenses are personal, and which you are obligated to pay for. Similar to the way the 50% must go toward essentials, the 30% is the maximum amount that you can allow to go towards personal expenses. The less you spend in this section, the more you will be able to pay down your debts and secure your future.

Continuing with the financial example, you have $1,650 to spend on this category. Everybody's wants are going to vary, but the main goal is to make sure that you don't dip into your savings money.

Establishing these good habits will last you a lifetime. You don't have to make thousands of dollars a week for this to work; anybody is able to follow this. Since this is percentage-based, you can apply the same proportion whether you have an entry-level salary, or if you are already years into your career.

A word of caution: it's important that you don't take this too literally. Everybody's life is a little bit different. This plan is here to provide you with a framework that you can work with. After you have reviewed your expenses and income, you have to figure out what's essential and what isn't. Then you can come up with a budget that will help you use your money more efficiently. Years later, you will be able to fall back on these guidelines so that your budget can evolve with your life.

A good software to look at is Mint, and it makes it easy to live by this budget. Once you have spent some time figuring out which expense fall into what section, you will be able to come up with your first budget and keep yourself on track. Your situation will change, and Mint will allow you to be able to adjust things when this happens.

Your Quick Start Action Step:

While the 50/20/30 budget is your goal, you're probably looking for something you can do right now or something you can see results in quickly. While what you must do right now is sit down to look at your spending, there are some other things that will help with your minimalist budget.

1. **Clean up**

    When your surroundings and senses are dominated by furniture and clothing, you will lose your ability to appreciate the things you have. Try using a vacuum cleaner, wiping up dust, and clearing out the trash—anything that you can do on a regular basis. Keeping a neat household will give you the ability to appreciate the things that you have bought—your chair, desk, bed, cooking wares, and so on will be easier seen once the clutter is gone.

2. **Take inventory, figure out the need, and donate**

    While you are cleaning up, think about the things that you actually need and what things are beneficial to you. If you find clothing that you haven't worn in the past year, maybe you can donate it. Do you have electronics or shoes that have been shoved in the corner for a rainy day? How often are you going to use it? What value does it bring? Also, if you need this motivation, donations will also give you a tax break.

3. **Create your budget**

    The time has come to bite the bullet, sit down, and come up with that budget. The only way a minimalist budget is going to help you is if you actually sit down and do it. Figure out your wants and needs and the money you bring in each month, and make that your starting point.

Chapter 8:
Recycling the Right Way While Still Making Money

8.1

Everybody has those closets, drawers, cabinets, and possibly rooms filled with things we just can't think about throwing away. We can't even get the energy to look at these items that may be both important and useless. This isn't even taking into account the personal items, like the drawer full of past cards from every occasion, stacks of unread books, dried up flowers from dates years ago, or crafts children made years ago that are falling apart.

There is no reason to hang onto paychecks, paid bills, contracts, or manuals from appliances that have been dead for years. All these stuff will weigh you down and will take up needed space. It will create emotional baggage and drama.

Once you begin throwing out old stuff like those manuals, contracts, paid bills, and paychecks, start crossing off things on that to-do list like running marathons or swimming the English Channel.

Decluttering isn't about just cleaning out your closet and desk. It's about getting rid of all the things you keep hanging onto from the past like unfinished business, relationships, and careers. It will be a big moment of power in your life.

Behind all that clutter is a thousand reasons why we hang onto things. You may read that stack of books one day. You may lose that weight and finally get back into those pants that have been in your closet since your college days. These items don't motivate us—they just fill us with shame and guilt. We *hope* we can one day read those books or fit into those clothes. When we don't, we begin to feel guilty. How much of one thing do you need to remind you of that moment in time? How many things must you hang onto until it begins to control your life?

We hold onto things thinking that we are going to need them. It is easy hiding things you don't need or use in a cabinet or closet. These things are going to pile up to a point where you won't be able to ignore them any longer. Even if it is in a closet behind closed doors, you are still hanging onto it. You have to figure out why this item is important instead of just shoving it under a rug.

8.2

Keeping your house clean can be a daunting task. Keeping it clean is important for a lot of reasons. These things can help you have a better life:

- You will do more. If your home gets disorganized or dirty, it may be hard to focus on what you need to do. You may get distracted by surface cleaning or trying to organize things. These will keep you from doing the important things. When your home is organized and clean, you will get more things done and have fewer distractions.

- You will be able to find things. If you are constantly losing your cell phone or keys, a clean house will simplify your life. You won't spend as much time looking for these misplaced items. Go through the mail when you get it. Get rid of papers you don't need or want. You are going to feel better once everything is organized.

- You will feel creative. A clean house lets your mind become creative and feel more relaxed. If you are surrounded by disorganization and uncleanliness, your mind will focus on the chaos, and your creative juices won't flow.

- You will have friends over. There isn't anything more embarrassing than inviting friends over, and your house is in shambles. This can make you stop inviting friends over. Don't let your house stop you from spending time with friends and loved ones. When you keep your home clean, you will invite more people into your home.

- It is good for your children. It isn't good for anybody of any age to live in filth. Young children who crawl are going to pick up everything on the floor and put it into their mouth. Children are susceptible to mildew, mold, and bacteria that can hurt their health. Keep your house sanitized and clean to keep your children healthy.

- You will have better sleep. There isn't a better feeling than jumping into a bed that has clean sheets and telling a clean house good night. You will rest better when you aren't waking up to chaos. Your mind will rest peacefully in a clean house.

8.3

Some stuff is easy to set aside, such as that company t-shirt that has holes in it and is too small or those birthday cards from several years ago. If you still have things like this, stop now and throw them out. Once you can get rid of things that are easy to identify, you can begin on the rest of the stuff. Let's find out what needs to stay and what needs to go:

1. **Sort it out:**

    You have to begin by sorting out all your excess. Put the items into categories that you can go through separately. These need to include gadgets, cables, clothing, and books. You can even be more specific if you have a problem collecting things for a hobby—things like sports equipment, photo albums, board games, and puzzles. These things can quickly accumulate at home. If something is taking up too much space, you need to find a category for it. With every category, sort the items into three piles: what you are keeping, what you are getting rid of, and what you aren't sure about. You have to get ruthless. When did you use that juicer? Are you going to use it later? Do you really need it? After you have sorted them all, go through all the piles you aren't certain about, and try to get rid of half of it. Now, it's time to put everything back. The things you are getting rid of goes into boxes, trash bags, or whatever you have decided to do with them just so they go out of the house. Now, the things you are keeping need to be put away nicely and neatly. Then, take a minute to admire all the new space you have created. Pick up the things you aren't sure about and place them somewhere. If it is clothing that needs hanging, hang it in a separate closet, or put it in a drawer. Don't put it together with what you are keeping. Keep track of what you will and will not use in the next 30 days. If you will use it, put it where it belongs. If you will not, get rid of it after the time limit is up.

2. **Repeat this step.**

Not right now. You have gotten rid of a lot of things you thought you cared about. You aren't in any emotional state to go through a bunch more possessions. Wait another 30 days, and do the process all over again.

There are several options when you want to get rid of stuff. You can donate, sell, or just trash them. Let's look at how you can do each of these things:

- Donating is an easy way to get rid of stuff you don't want. Finding a local Goodwill or Salvation Army are good places to start. There may also be other charities in your area that run thrift stores to help them run their charities such as Brother Wolf or a local animal shelter. You can even have an open house party where you invite your friends for some food and fun, and then they get to go through your stuff and take home things they want.

- Selling is a great way to get rid of your things and make some money, too. The easiest way to start is eBay or Craigslist. Craigslist is great for large items you can't ship like furniture. You may decide to sell all your things through Craigslist, especially if you don't want the hassle of shipping. eBay is great if you have collectibles you want to sell, though.

- Most of the stuff in your house may fit into a hard drive if you put in some effort. If you have old photos or VHS tapes, putting these things on digital hard drives will save you a bunch of money.

- Throwing things out is the easiest of all since you probably already have trash bags on hand. Fill up the bag with things that you can't or don't want to sell, and take it to the curb. Throwing things out isn't easy, but you need to do it safely. Technology doesn't need to go to the landfill. If it can be recycled, take it to a recycler. Check out Gazelle to see if they want your old electronics.

3. **Get rid of unused sports equipment.**

Yes, I completely believe you when you said you were going to use that mini trampoline to jump on every day, and I'm sure you were going to incorporate some amazing workouts with those pretty pink free weights.

Let's be honest with ourselves: none of that actually happened, and now, your cabinets are filled up with retired sporting equipment. When it comes to getting rid of stuff, you have to be completely honest with yourself. Ask, "Am I really going to ever use this stuff?"

4. **"Acquired" mini hotel toiletries.**

Everybody gets excited when they stay at a hotel and see all those little toiletries. Then, you realize you have a box full of travel-size soaps that won't ever get used. Unless you are planning on going camping, or you have a lot of guests who are going to stay with you, these are things that must definitely be gotten rid of.

5. **Throw out things such as bread makers.**

    Do you really need that bread maker? All of these clunky machines are just taking up a bunch of important space in your home. They are just gathering dust, and they aren't really necessary. If you do actually make your own bread, you can use your oven and clear out a big spot in your kitchen.

6. **Throw out things that you don't ever play.**

    Did anybody in your household believe they were going to learn how to play the guitar but then lost interest? Has the expensive electric drum kit turned into a clothes hanger?

    Learning to get rid of things that you've had full intention of using can be pretty hard—but if you've not actually used it at this point, you probably ever won't. Take that plunge, and get rid of those things to free up some space.

7. **Crazy pizza gadgets**

    All of those snazzy pizza makers and those neat little pizza cutting shears looked like amazing tools, and you thought they were a good idea. But when did you last use them? Unless you make a pizza once or more each week, then you probably don't really need any of those items taking up space in your kitchen.

8. **Throw out everything that is already broken.**

    Why are you still holding onto things that are broken? If you can fix the broken items, then fix them; otherwise, just throw them away. You can also donate them or sell them to junk shops. There are some artists that will use donated toys to make things, so you can browse through some of the local boards before you throw the items away.

9. **Throw out all of those old cookbooks.**

    The old cookbooks may look pretty, but do you really use them all that much? If you don't use them often, then it's probably a good idea to get rid of them. It can be extremely hard to get rid of things that you are fond of, but there are also plenty of online resources for you to use when it comes to finding a new recipe to cook—and these take up much less space. You can print out your favorite recipes and then put them in a three-ring binder. That way, you have only one cookbook, and it only has recipes that you actually cook.

10. **Throw out your old receipts.**

    Chances are, if you check your coat pockets, wallets, or bags—you are going to find at least one receipt in them. Let's be honest: how many times have you pulled a coat out to wear at the beginning of winter that you haven't worn since last winter, and you stick your hand in the pocket and pull out a chunk of receipts and tissues?

    Gather them all up, and then glance through them before you get rid of them to make sure that you have accounted for all those things. This may help you realize that you are spending too much money on certain things. Learning how to throw away things on a regular basis will help you stay more organized and reduce your clutter.

11. Get rid of your old magazines.

Having some magazines around the house for guests is a nice thing, but chances are that you aren't going to read those out-of-date magazines ever again, so it's a good idea to recycle them. You can even try to donate those magazines to local libraries or doctor's offices. Before you allow these things to pile up in your house, see if there is something that you can do with them first.

12. Get rid of your old pillows.

Throwing out things like pillows tend to be rather tricky because they aren't cheap, but you think they are going to last a lifetime. In order to figure out if you need to get a new pillow, try this:

Fold the pillow in half, if it easily stays in this folded position, then you need to get a new pillow.

Your body and hair oils penetrate the pillow while you sleep, and this will start to change the color of the pillow. It will then become a breeding ground for dust mites and other odor-causing bacteria. You can often donate these old pillows to pet shelters. They will use them for pet beds.

13. Get rid of the jewelry you no longer wear or have never worn.

Go through your jewelry box and see if there are any pieces that you don't wear anymore—worse yet if you have any that you haven't taken out of their box or their packaging. You may find a bunch of jewelry that you don't wear or haven't even worn. You can choose to donate the jewelry, or you can try to sell them and get some extra money put into your savings.

14. **Throw out clothes that you don't ever wear.**

    This is especially true if you are trying to lose weight. Don't hold onto that size-six pair of jeans just in case you are able to fit back in them. Chances are, if you make it back down to that size, you are going to want to buy new clothes instead of wearing old ones. Another great trick is that every time you wear an article of clothing, flip the clothes hanger around so that you know you have worn it recently. Then every six months to a year, go through your closet and get rid of clothes that hanger hasn't been moved.

15. **Recycle those old boxes.**

    You may believe that you are being organized by holding onto those old product boxes like a cell phone or TV packaging, but the only thing you are doing is taking up space in your house. Instead, place the details and leaflets that you need inside a folder. This will save you space, and you will be able to find them more easily if you ever need them.

Your Quick Start Action Step:

When trying to figure out where to start when decluttering, begin with the room that bothers you the most. You may get an overwhelming feeling when you start because you have just too much clutter. These tips will help you get started:

- When you begin organizing one area, begin by throwing away the trash.

    Every room in a house is going to have trash in it. Look for broken pieces, expired coupons, empty containers, and dried-up glue. Getting rid of the trash first will help you concentrate on the rest of the clutter.

- For some unknown reason, all things wind up in the kitchen.

Before you begin arranging your cabinets, get things that don't belong in the kitchen out of it. Make a pile of things that go into other rooms. Make sure you make a pile for each room. Take the appropriate things to the right rooms, and leave them there.

Something that most people don't think about checking is their spice rack. Head to your kitchen and go through your spices to check their expiration dates. You may be shocked to see that you have quite a few out-of-date spices.

Once you've gone through your spices, head to your cupboard and have a look at the best-by dates on your bottles of sauces. Anything that you find that is out-of-date, get rid of it. Anything that you find that is getting close to the best-by date, position them at the front of your cabinet so that you know that they need to be used first.

Training yourself to do these on a regular basis will help you to save some time in the future.

You're not done in the kitchen just yet. Check to see if you have any plastic silverware. Look to see if you have any of those plastic bags of fork, knife, and napkin. Unless you entertain a lot of people or you eat on the go, you aren't going to need these things cluttering up your drawers. You probably already have proper silverware as well. Recycle these items.

While you're at it, get rid of condiment packets. Nobody ever uses the extra packets of ketchup. Buy a full-size bottle of the stuff and use it. It takes up a lot less space.

While you are cleaning out your fridge, get rid of leftovers that have been in there for more than five days. Throw out any food storage containers that have missing pieces. That missing lid isn't going to turn up, so just throw away the bowl.

- All magazines and reading materials end up in the living room.

It gets moved around all over the place when you look for the remote. It might end up outdated, dusty, spilled on, and bent. It becomes something nobody wants to see. This can be eliminated when you can straighten up the piles of papers. A nice and neat pile looks like it is supposed to be there.

- Work on your bathroom one shelf or drawer at a time.

Throw out all items that have been used up or expired. Some medicines are still effective, but you are trying to declutter. The important thing to remember is that there are right and wrong ways to get rid of these things. You don't want to just toss them down the drain or into your garbage can. You can even contact a pharmacy for suggestions if you need to, but there are a lot of resources online.

- The home office is bad at holding onto bunches of clutter.

Get rid of items that you aren't working on anymore. Begin with stuff you have tried to keep until you find the part you need. If it hasn't been found by now, it never will. If you have no idea where a cord goes to, toss it. If you have newspapers that are more than two days old, get rid of them. Also, do you really need that rubber band ball?

Get a scrap piece of paper, and test all of your pens. Throw out those that don't work. Most people don't bother buying refills for pens, so there's no sense in keeping a pen that you've already replaced.

Get rid of last year's calendar. People hang onto calendars for a myriad of reason. The two biggest are that they think the pictures in it are cute, or that they are going to transfer important dates to their new calendar. Keep the calendar until January 31st, and if you haven't done anything with it by that time, toss it.

There is a constant theme throughout. Begin with obvious trash, lower the volume of materials, and focus on what is left in the area one section at a time.

Chapter 9:
The "Less is More" Lifestyle for Debt-Free and Stress-Free Living

9.1

Being debt-free is a great feeling. Getting to this point is very hard. What's even harder is staying free of debt.

It can be done with dedication and hard work. Getting control of your money and controlling how and where you spend it is priceless.

In today's society, being in debt is normal. When someone says they have gotten and stayed out of debt, it is just too crazy for most people to believe. You are definitely swimming upstream. But the big question is: is it worth it?

- Sacrifice is empowering: You may have to work more than one job, and trudge through a job that you don't really like—but knowing you are going to come out a winner will make it worth it. Becoming debt-free means you will have financial freedom, inner peace, and obviously more money. There are other benefits as well. The largest advantage of sacrificing and getting to your goal is knowing you have followed through and are able to reap the rewards. When you have to face a hard life choice or financial problem, you will know that you have the ability to handle whatever is thrown at you.

- Being financially free may get boring. Before you get rid of your debt, making decisions can consist of complicated strategies and many questions like: do I take a vacation, pay off the credit card, what do I pay first, and what card has the highest interest rate? Decisions are a lot easier. Pay the bills, put extra money into investing or savings, and use any money left over for other goals or entertainment. When you are debt-free, making decisions is a bit boring. You won't have any complicated spreadsheets. You are just living within your budget. If you absolutely love living on the edge, you will see when you have complete control over your finances that your life isn't as much exciting anymore. Slow and steady really does win the race. In this world of crazy financial ventures and endless promotions, the road to freedom is really boring.

- Getting back into debt is easy. You may soon see that your life after the debt is boring. Everything you encounter tempts you to spend more, and you find it hard to say no. This is very true when you have paid off all your credit cards, and they are upping your credit limit constantly. It is crazy to think it is super easy to put a few charges on your credit card, and then all of a sudden you are thousands of dollars in debt. There are some credit cards with good deals if you absolutely can't live without one. Some credit cards give you thousands of airline miles for charging a specific amount each month. If you can pay these off quickly, this is a great way to get free plane tickets. Even if you are disciplined enough to get out of debt, you must be disciplined enough to stay out. Just because you have everything paid off, doesn't mean you won't get the urge to buy things.

- It will feel like an uphill battle. Many people don't talk about life without debt, but it is like a slap in the face when reality kicks in. Just going to the store and buying groceries may scare you to death. You may constantly wonder if you have spent too much. The constant fear of going back into debt will creep into your mind. You have worked very hard to get free from debt, but you may realize that living a life without debt in it is very hard. It is an uphill battle constantly. You will still have moments where you wonder if you are going to be able to pay your bills or if you can actually afford that trip you promised the kids. Then the old worry about making enough money creeps into your mind. It doesn't matter if you are living your life after a debt or just trying to pay off your debts—you have to spend money in order to survive. This means that it will be a day-to-day struggle. The economy doesn't worry about the people who are trying to find their financial path without being in debt. The economy isn't nice to people who are trying to swim upstream. Then life hits you with these questions:

- Will I really be able to save money?
- Will it be enough?
- Will I ever have true financial freedom from creditors and banks?

- Will it be worth it? Even though you have all these questions going through your head and struggle with them each day, you are still going to live a life free from debt. You don't let banks or creditors control your life—you control it. It doesn't matter how scary this may sound; it should fill your heart with hope.

- The truth about life after the debt is that once the excitement of being debt-free wears off, you will find there are downsides to being debt-free. Most people don't talk about it. So what is this downside? It is the fear of going back into debt. Everywhere you turn, you are going to encounter loan or credit card applications being thrown at you. People are going to try to persuade you to spend money you don't want to. It will get overwhelming. Society, in general, is geared to being in debt and staying there for their entire lives. It is a daily struggle to remain debt-free since this idea isn't normal in mainstream life. People are going to look at you like you have two heads when you constantly say no. Knowing you are going to have financial freedom and will be able to overcome all financial obstacles will give you all sorts of possibilities to have a life that is worth living free from debt. This sort of freedom will be totally worth it.

9.2

You may be wondering what the benefits of paying off your debts are. The most common are: freedom to spend the money any way you want, not having to live paycheck-to-paycheck, and having more money available in your accounts. Are there other benefits to being free from debt? Yes, there are. Here are some great benefits to being debt-free:

- No more mental and physical stress: When you are dealing with huge amounts of debt, you may realize that you have many health problems. Four major health problems come from stress. These are lower respiratory problems, cancer, stroke, and heart disease. The biggest factor is your financial stress. When you can pay your debt down, you are going to reduce your mental and physical stressors. This will help you become a happier and healthier person.

- Relationships will be better: Most people who fight or end up divorced say the reason behind it was almost always money. When you can reduce your debt, you are getting rid of the largest factor that causes stress in a relationship. Studies have shown that couples who are happy in their marriage do live longer than unhappy married people, divorced people, and single people. Less or no debt will mean you have less to fight about. This will lead to a more harmonious relationship. Your relationship will be more successful, plus you will find the relationship with your parents and children will also improve.

- Funding your dreams will be attainable: Getting rid of debt gives you an opportunity to give, save, and spend the way you want to. You will finally be able to have that dream vacation you've always wanted. You may need new furniture—guess what? You can now go out and buy what you want. Achieving financial freedom allows you and your money to have your goals and dreams, instead of making somebody else's account bigger. You are no longer in debt to creditors for the rest of your life. You will be able to have fun and take risks.

- You will finally have peace of mind. Having this is absolutely priceless.

There is nothing in the world better than having peace of mind. When you lay down at night and you know that you can take care of your family, that you can send your child to the college of their dreams, and that your job is the one you truly love—these benefits are easily attainable when you aren't in debt. You may not see them on paper, but life is more than just a math problem. When you start paying off your debts, you may experience these great side effects.

9.3

Most of this debt you have accumulated was for nothing. It just financed a short-lived lifestyle that vanished in a couple of years. Why does this happen? Most people believe that in order to live a modern life, you have to be in debt to do it.

Here are a few things that you can start doing now to help you gain control of your finances:

- Don't buy things you will forget quickly. If what you want to do or buy is something that you will just forget in a week, it isn't worth spending the money on. The only things you need to spend money on are your essential basic needs like shelter, clothing, and food. You may like doing memorable events such as having coffee each morning with friends—but you do this every day until it just isn't that enjoyable anymore. It has become normal and totally forgettable. Now, you are faced with an added expense where you are completely throwing money down the drain. Special purchases may even become totally forgettable. That book you have looked forward to reading is special but what about the 20th one? It is just put on the shelf with the rest.

- Look at your financial statement and find these unnecessary purchases. Did you make any purchases that you don't even remember making? Look for where you have spent the most money, and realize these are very wasteful purchases. Stay away from such places.

- Stay away from foods that are convenient. There is absolutely nothing wrong with taking your significant other out to a nice restaurant if it is for a memorable occasion like an anniversary or getting together with friends you haven't seen in a long time. It becomes a problem when you are just running short of time and swing into a drive-thru just to save you some time. These meals become totally forgettable. These meals are completely unhealthy, expensive, and really don't even save you much time. This also holds true for gas stations and convenience stores. You may be extremely thirsty or hungry when taking a road trip. This is why packing some snacks and drinks is so important.

- Take public transportation when you can. This isn't saying you must not own a car. Everybody has different living situations, and some may *need* a car. If you live in a rural area, you pretty much need a car to get places. If it is possible, your mode of transportation can be something that isn't as expensive as a car. A car must be a backup. What are these other modes of transportation? They are your feet, your bicycle, and public transportation. Cars can get expensive, even when they are paid for in full. There is parking, gas, maintenance, registration, and insurance. These can add up fast. If you can live without a car, you will be better off. If you absolutely need to have a car, think about buying a used one. Drive it until it is falling apart, then swap it for another used one.

- Go to the local library for entertainment. Most people think a local library is a place with angry librarians that tell everybody to hush. It is just row after row of dusty shelves full of old books. Obviously, they haven't been inside a library in an extremely long time. Libraries today have books for every reader, including children and adults. You will find educational books and page turners in every genre you can imagine. They even have DVDs of every genre as well. Some will have audiobooks available as well as equipment you can borrow. The great news here is it is all free. You only have to pay if you turn them in late. When you get tempted to rent or buy an audiobook, DVD, or book, check out your local library instead especially if you aren't sure you if are going to like it. Rent it for free before spending the money to buy it.

- Outdoor hobbies can serve many purposes. It gets you out and moving. This is great for your health. You are going to feel better, keep your medical problems away, and have more energy. Many outdoor hobbies aren't expensive. You are just going to need shoes and some time—and perhaps some equipment like soccer or other types of balls. Another reason for outdoor hobbies is that they are very social. You can become a part of a ball team and make new friends. You may even start collecting things like rocks, shells, or photographs. I have a close friend who collects heart-shaped rocks when she goes hiking with her grandchildren. I love taking pictures of nature that I put into calendars for presents.

Your Quick Start Action Step:

When you get out of debt, it is very tempting to start spending again. You are going to start getting all sorts of preapproved credit cards in the mail. Throw these in the trash. Track your spending. Just because you don't have any debt, doesn't mean you can spend your money without thinking about it. You don't necessarily have to stick to a strict budget. You do have to monitor your spending. By doing this, you will keep a feel for your spending. Once you get into the habit of looking through your financial statements, you will be able to feel that you are spending too much money.

A key for success in living free from debt is to change your expectations. Adopt a mentality where the money you are saving is worth more to you than that item you think you can't live without. You don't need the newest model of smartphone. You've only had the one you've gotten for a couple of months. Use it until it starts messing up, then trade in for a newer model. Each time you check your savings account, and it has gained interest, this must excite you more than buying that new computer or those new shoes that you really don't need.

Appreciate what you have. This is a very important step. Look around you, and take pride in what you possess. Look at your computer, television, furniture, car, and house. Now, look at nonphysical things like electricity, heat, air conditioning, and wireless network. As long as your health is good, you have the world. There is so much in life that you can look forward to. It doesn't matter how poor you feel right now—think about the less fortunate people in third world countries that would give anything to experience what you have right now. Being happy doesn't necessarily mean spending a lot of money. Just focus on what you have now and treasure them.

Bonus Chapter: Tips on Dealing with Large Expenses

10.1

In this day and age, financial tips are needed to stick to a budget and save money. When we are faced with a lot of information, we start asking the common question: "Where do I start?" For many, there are five areas that will take over 50 percent of our money. This is the best place to start.

These areas are retirement, education, children, car, and home. Let's see what we need to do:

- You need to feed a retirement fund. The amount of money you need to put aside to be able to retire is based on a simple equation of taking your current yearly income and multiply by 25. If your take-home pay for the year is $60,000, and you want to be able to still live comfortably off that—you are going to need a retirement fund of $1,500,000. If you know this number early in your career, this will help you realize the importance of having this savings plan.

- Do you have to ask yourself how much is too much for a good education? People used to think it was fine to be in debt for student loans and a mortgage. Any other debt was considered bad debt. This isn't true now. We have figured out that too much of anything is actually bad. One rule of thumb is to not accrue more education debt than you will earn in the first ten years after you have graduated from both college and graduate school. Basically, if you know your job is going to give you around $60,000 a year, never exceed this amount in student loans. The logic here is that if it is going to take you over ten years to pay ten percent of your income each year in repaying loans, it will be hard to pay your other bills.

- Children can be expensive. The Department of Agriculture has estimated that it costs around $220,000 to raise a child from diapers to the age of 18.

This is before the cost of education we listed above. Making the decision of becoming a parent is a large financial obligation.

- Your vehicles can drive you into a poor house. Many can usually afford to have a car that is about one-third of their total income for the year. If you make $50,000, you can easily have a car that costs $16,500. This may seem low, but this is why most people have financial problems. They drive it every day. Cars have a lot of other costs other than the monthly payment. You have to pay for maintenance, parking, gas, insurance, and many others. If you want to save money, the cost of transportation needs to be ten percent or lower of your annual income.

- How much of a house will you be able to comfortably afford? Many people use the rule of thumb where the purchase price of their home doesn't cost more than three times their yearly income. Maintaining a home is more than just your mortgage payment. You also have the upkeep, insurance, and property tax. These things can run you another two to three percent of the cost of your home every year. If you put 20 percent down on a 30-year fixed mortgage, your interest rate is around five to six percent, then three times your income will turn to about 30 percent of your total yearly income.

10.2

Cost of living is how much money you are going to need to live within a certain means. This includes healthcare, taxes, food, and housing. Most people use cost of living to figure out if they will be able to live in a certain city as opposed to another one. This is connected to your wages since salary is a measure of what is needed to keep up your normal mode of living in certain geographic regions.

Cost of living is a major factor when talking about accumulating personal wealth since a small salary can go further in cities where everything is relatively cheaper. If you have a larger salary, you may be able to live in a bigger, more expensive city. In a 2015 cost of living survey, the most expensive cities to live in were New York City, Copenhagen, Zurich, Hong Kong, Geneva, Moscow, Osaka, and Tokyo. Cities within the United States that had the highest cost of living were San Francisco, Washington, Los Angeles, and Honolulu.

10.3

Creating a monthly budget usually makes sense. You have to set aside money to pay for student loans, utilities, mortgage or rent, and all the other bills you have, right? The big problem with some expenses like that vacation you want to take at the end of the school year, your friend's wedding in Aruba, and shopping for holidays only come up occasionally (like, once a year).

How can you put them into your monthly budget? Use these guidelines to help you stay on track:

- Plan Ahead: At the start of every year, sit down and plan when you are going to take your vacation days. Most people only have a specific number available each year. Planning a budget is similar. If you already know you are going to your friend's wedding, allocate money for the cost of the dress, plane tickets, wedding gifts, and miscellaneous expenses once you get there. You have to figure out how much you need to save. Take this number and divide it by the number of paychecks you will get before then. This will tell you how much you need to take out of each check to cover this expense. Let's not forget the expenses you have every year like car insurance. If you pay the entire premium when it comes due every six months, you can budget the amount out of each check to cover that cost as well.

- Figure Out Places to Save: After you have figured out the amount of money you need to get you through the year, you can look into some options. If you are good at keeping track of your budget, it is perfectly fine to put the money you need to save each month into a separate account and transfer it over when you need to pay a bill. It may be better to create different accounts for every expense like a holiday fund, computer fund, or vacation fund. This way, you can keep track of how much you have set aside for each and if you are reaching your target. Check with your financial institution, and see if they offer accounts such as a Christmas Club that will help you stay honest. You can put money into it all through the year; it penalizes you if you take money out before a specific date.

- Emergency Account: You need to put money into an emergency account for just that—emergencies. This will keep you from having to drain another account if you are faced with an unexpected expense. Some experts recommend having the amount of around three to six months of your total living expenses if you have an emergency such as repairs to your house or car, hospital stays, or losing a job. It may be tempting to tap into this account but *don't*. This money is *only* for emergencies. If you start skimming a little bit of money from this account here and there, you may find yourself in big trouble if an emergency were to actually arise.

- Don't Use Credit Cards: This is like dipping into the emergency account. A credit card can become a threat to your finances. It is okay to place a big purchase on a card to get you those airline miles, rewards, or even cash back—but you need to be sure you have put this into your monthly budget. You need to make sure you can pay it off in just a couple of months. If you begin paying interest each month, that wonderful deal will cost you a lot more than you have budgeted for.

When you plan ahead for all your expenses—including the less common and larger ones—you will be able to feel secure in knowing that you have the money to cover everything.

Your Quick Start Action Step

Put your plans on a calendar. You don't head out on vacation without knowing exactly where you are going. You need to do the same for your money. Get a calendar and sit down with your spouse or significant other, and put any irregular expenses you think you may encounter this year on it. These may include holidays, school supplies, tag renewals, vacation, and insurance. Write down how much you will need for each, and put this figure on the calendar when it will be due.

Once you know what to expect, you now need to put these into your budget monthly. For every expense, divide how much you need by how many months you have until the payment is due. Add this result to your monthly budget. You may have realized that when your load is light, it is easier to move around. The same goes for your finances. If your expenses are small, your money will go further. It seems worthwhile to find ways to cut down your expenses.

Insurance premiums are always a large amount of money that comes up usually every six months. Many insurance companies offer ways to save your money if you bundle your home and auto insurance together at the same premium. This can save you hundreds of dollars every six months.

The hardest part of planning a budget is figuring out how much money you need to set aside for unexpected expenses. Once you practice this awhile, it will become natural. Just use the tips above, and you will soon find you have more money than you realize.

Conclusion

Now that you've read *Minimalist Budget: How to Achieve Financial Success & Solve Debt with Simple Money Strategies to Positively Transform and Simplify Your Life*, you are well prepared to overhaul your spending habits with a proactive and optimistic mindset for your future. The key to creating a minimalist budget is to rewire your thinking from the lack of cash flow and resources. This way of thinking haunts most Americans whenever a bill or financial emergency strikes to a grounded and value-based mindset that will steer you confidently in the direction of your dreams. Your budget must reflect your true values, both in the short-term and long-term. Making daily spending choices that are influenced by your authentic self will free you from that icky, guilt-ridden feeling of buyer's remorse—or worse, the dull pang of knowing you must have been paying better attention to your finances. Life is never about money, and this book explores the very human dilemma of how to both provide for your lifestyle while investing in your future. The great reward is finding your true power, not in possessions and extraneous expenses, but in yourself. No matter how dire your financial situation is, no matter how impossible it may seem to get yourself out of your financial hole, no matter how many times friends and family members may have written you off as a lost cause—you are not alone, and you can fully financially recover. The step-by-step instructions at the end of each chapter will guide you and immediately impact your financial health for the better. Set yourself free from debt and worry by embracing the power you have to choose to live simply, smartly, and with the *Minimalist Budget* mindset.

Finally, if this book has given you value and has helped you in any way, then I'd like to ask you for a favor if you would be kind enough to leave a review for this book on Amazon? It'd be greatly appreciated!

Thank you and good luck!

Preview Of 'Declutter Your Mind' by Marie S. Davenport

Chapter 3: Why your Mind is Filled with Clutter - And How to Fix It

3.1 Your brain on clutter

Described as anything that is kept, even though not used, needed or wanted, clutter can also be defined as having a disorganized and overwhelming amount of possessions in our living space, cars or storage areas. But clutter isn't just physical. When you have to-do items constantly floating around in your head, or you hear a ring every few minutes from your phone, your brain doesn't get a chance to fully enter creative flow or process experiences. Clutter creates stress that has three major biological and neurological effects on us—our cortisol levels, our creativity and ability to focus, and our experience of pain.

The overconsumption of digital stuff—like social media notifications, news feeds, games and files on our computer—competes for our attention, creating a digital form of clutter that has the same effect on our brain as physical clutter. Neatness and order support health—and oppose chaos.

So, what is going on? Our brains love order. The human body consists of thousands of integrated and interdependent biological and neurochemical systems, all organized and operating along circadian rhythms, without which our bodies would disintegrate into chaos. It's no wonder that the organization within our very own bodies naturally extends to the desire for order and tidiness in our homes. And order feels good, in part, because it's easier for our brains to deal with and not have to work so hard.

3.2 The science of cortisol

No matter the ways, reasons, and means by which the creep of stuff exceeds our ability to mentally and physically manage it—all of it amounts to stress. Clutter can trigger the release of the stress hormone cortisol, which can increase tension and anxiety and lead to unhealthy habits. Cortisol is a hormone produced in response to stress by the hypothalamus-pituitary-adrenal axis (HPA).

Chronic clutter can create prolonged stress, throwing us into a state of low-grade, perpetual fight-or-flight—the system designed to help us survive. The fight-or-flight response involves the complex interaction of many body systems and organs that activate needed functions and minimize unnecessary functions during times of stress. These systems must remain in balance to maintain optimum physical and psychological health.

According to a Cornell University study from 2016, stress triggered by clutter may also trigger coping and avoidance strategies, like eating junk food, oversleeping or binge-watching Netflix.

If we are not stressed, we get most of our cortisol in the morning to get us going. Levels taper off the rest of the day if we are relaxed, enabling us to enjoy psychological and physical wellbeing. But a messy home environment can prevent our body's cortisol levels from naturally declining throughout the day. Taxing this system eventually results in higher levels of depression and anxiety, and a lower capacity to think clearly, make decisions, and stay focused.

To supply the body with the energy needed to deal with stress, there are several physiological changes that occur with elevated cortisol levels:

- Diversion of blood flow to the muscles from other parts of the body

- Increased blood pressure
- Increased heart rate
- Increased blood sugars
- Increased fats in in the blood

If there is no relief from stress, all of these changes are bad for healthy brain activity and can cause lasting negative changes in brain function and structure. Additionally, when stress raises the body's cortisol levels, its overall health can be adversely affected, including organ damage, the suppression of the immune, endocrine and reproductive systems, the lowering of the metabolism, and the disruption of the sleep cycle, to name a few.

It is difficult to maintain a state of wellness over time when the body's energy is channeled into coping with stress.

Just as concerning, when the body is in a state of chronic stress and not thinking clearly, the brain tends to only see that which is negative as these are, historically, the things that could turn into threats. Unfortunately, all this does is reinforce the pre-existing sour point of view, perceived lack of social support and subsequent poor interrelationships.

Research from a 2009 study out of UCLA's Center on Everyday Lives of Families (CELF) has shown that women who perceive their homes to be cluttered tend to have unhealthy patterns of cortisol levels. A team of professional archaeologists, anthropologists, and other social scientists studied the home life of 32 middle-class, dual-income families with 2-3 children of ages 7-12 in Los Angeles. In the study, family members recorded self-directed home tours describing objects and spaces in their homes, during which saliva samples were taken at regular intervals to measure cortisol levels.

The data were collected for three days and compared to and correlated with vast amounts of other data previously collected over the course of four years. According to the CEFL study, the amount of stress women experience at home is directly proportional to the amount of stuff they and their family had accumulated.

It's interesting to note in the UCLA study that men did not exhibit the same results, having normal cortisol fluctuations. Presumably, they were not as stressed by the amount of stuff in their home. This can be explained possibly by the results of other studies that have shown that the home is traditionally perceived as women's domain and ultimate responsibility, even in households where both partners work.

Other studies also support the finding that if men don't think the responsibility of keeping the house tidy is relevant to them, they may not be inclined to see the clutter and so are not as stressed about it.

This may be explained further in part by research that has indicated that there are distinct differences in vision between men and women since men have 25 percent more neurons in their visual cortex, a part of the cerebral cortex that processes visual information. The irony is that even though the visual cortex of a man has more neurons than a woman's, men are impacted more by the things they see that they think have to do with them, and less by the things they think do not.

The brain has a limited capacity to process information. To filter out extra stimuli and focus on what we are trying to achieve at any given moment, the top-down and bottom-up attention mechanisms compete. By mutually suppressing each other, brain power is exhausted, and ultimately, we lose focus. Whether we know it or not, a kitchen counter stacked with mail and basket full of unfolded laundry can be as distracting to us as a toddler in the throes of a tantrum.

3.3 **Start to declutter**

Now that we know what all of our extra stuff is doing to our health and ability to function, it's time to get rid of it, right?... Oh, but if it were only that easy. Although most people don't experience heightened ACC/Insula activity to this degree, we can all identify with the feeling of angst when finally tossing that pile of unread magazines, or those ticket stubs from last summer's trip to New York to see Hamilton. The good news is, those who suffer from hoarding respond well to Cognitive Behavioral Therapy. For the rest of us... there is decluttering.

In addition to improving your mood and focus, decluttering often acts as a catalyst for taking better care of other aspects of our life. By purging unneeded items from our homes, it is like deleting files to create disk space on your computer. Suddenly, the whole operating system is more efficient...this decreases stress and increases your effectiveness personally and professionally.

While actually going ahead and getting rid of unnecessary items will be covered in detail in a later chapter, the exercises in this chapter are going to cover the preparation you will need to do in order to get ready to declutter once and for all. This lifestyle change requires two things: a vision list, and a why list. You will want to start with your vision list. This list is going to be everything you want to accomplish from your future results. Your list can, and should, contain anything that is important to you and serves as a reason for why you are making this lifestyle change. The more unique and personal this list is, the better it will serve you.

If you are having a hard time getting started, here are some things you might consider writing on your vision list:
- I want to eat healthier at every single meal
- I want to experience the loving relationships in my life, every day
- I want to contribute to the world in a meaningful way, daily
- I want to read and write on a daily basis
- I want to be passionate about every single day that I'm alive
- I want to take risks in life
- I want to be present in every single moment

These visions are essentially what you want to accomplish through your minimalist lifestyle. After you are clear on what you want to achieve with your new lifestyle, you want to get clear on why. Understanding why you want change is what will compel you to actually make the change. So, after you completely your list that outlines everything you want, you can start a list right beneath it that is going to tell you every reason why you want it. You should make sure that both lists are as detailed as possible. If you have several important items on your vision list, and on your why list, that is completely okay. You should not feel as though you have to limit yourself. The more reasons you can provide, the easier the entire transition is going to be for you.

As you become more aware of what you want, as well as why you want it you should find that it becomes easier and easier to motivate yourself to actually start working towards achieving your dreams. While you may feel as though your good intentions are strong enough to get you through right now, not listening to your mental clutter can be more difficult at the moment than you might expect. That is why it is important to have your vision and your why. These are lists you will refer back to when you are feeling internal resistances. You can regroup, refocus, and start all over again in a new frame of mind that will allow you to have an easier ability to achieve your desired results.

Your Quick Start Action Step: Start working on your vision list

As discussed above, your vision list is the linchpin that holds your motivation together. You don't need to put it together all at once, however, if you need some time to work on it that is perfectly fine. You can keep a running tally of things to add to it whenever you think of a new one. This process doesn't have to stop either, you can add something new to your vision list whenever the need strikes you.

Chapter 4: Effective Meditation - Being in the Present Moment

4.1 An ancient practice

Mindfulness meditation is a type of meditation which focuses on being as aware of each moment as possible, thereby helping the consciousness to expand by forming a stronger connection with the present. Mindfulness meditation has a long history of practice as part of the Buddhist faith where it is revered for its ability to improve both mental happiness and physical well-being. This has been corroborated by research which shows that mindfulness meditation is a beneficial treatment for a variety of mental conditions. What's more, it has also been shown to be effective when treating conditions including anxiety, stress and drug addiction.

While mindfulness can be practiced almost anywhere at nearly any time, the concept began as a structured meditation technique practiced by Buddhists known as vipassana. Roughly translated this means to live in the moment while understanding that sometimes you must be aware of the future as well. The general idea is that achieving vipassana will allow you to come to understand the universe as a whole and comes through the knowing of a few key principals.

The idea of practicing mindfulness first caught on in the Western world in the early part of the 1970s. Professor Jon Kabat-Zinn is credited with creating a mindfulness based method of stress reduction which paired mindfulness with yoga to great result. While Zinn didn't do anything particularly new, the fact that his techniques led to measurable improvements for a wide variety of ailments both mental and physical in turn led to additional studies on the topic. These studies have shown time and again how effective practicing mindfulness can be which in turn has led to a steady increase in the practice to the point where it can now be found being regularly practiced in schools, veteran treatment facilities, hospitals, even prisons.

4.2 Many benefits

In addition to helping improve self-discipline, studies show that that taking 15 minutes out of your day to practice mindfulness meditation has a host of additional benefits as well. For starters, it is known to show dramatic increases when it comes to projecting a strong sense of self while at the same time noticeably reducing stress. This is thanks to the positive effects that mindfulness meditation has on attention span, emotional regulation and body awareness. What's even more impressive, neuroimaging has shown that mindfulness meditation actually allows those who practice it to process information more quickly than those who do not.

The activity can also literally improve the health of the brain as studies show that those who started practicing mindfulness meditation at a young age actually have more volume in their brains as they age. Meditating regularly is also known to increase the thickness of the hippocampus which means that it actually makes it easier to learn new information and retain it for a prolonged period of time. It also positively affects the amygdala which means those who meditate are less likely to experience stress, anxiety, and fear. With so much going on under the hood, is it any wonder that those who meditate tend to report an overall increase in mood, temperament, and wellbeing?

Beyond these noticeable physical changes, regularly practicing mindfulness is known to help improve self-discipline in additional ways by decreasing instances of meditators' minds getting stuck in negative thought patterns while also making it easier to focus for prolonged periods of time. A recent Johns Hopkins University study found that practicing mindfulness meditation regularly is equally effective at treating anxiety, depression, and ADHD as many commonly prescribed drugs.

Other reasons to practice mindfulness meditation

- Mindfulness meditation naturally leads to a deeper understanding of the self and allows many people to take stock of their strengths and weaknesses, leading to personal growth.
- Studies show that those who practice mindfulness regularly have a stronger memory, leading to an easier retention of facts in both the long and the short term.

- In addition to the specifics, mindfulness meditation improves overall physical wellbeing with those who practice regularly reporting fewer instances of illness and a more rapid recovery when they do fall ill.

- Mindfulness meditation can help improve emotional control while at the same time increasing one's threshold for pain.

- As surprising as it might seem, making a habit of being mindful can actually make even the most middling music seem more engaging. This deeper level of engagement leads to a general increase of enjoyment, regardless of the type of music or any previous musical preferences.

- With a regular dose of mindfulness meditation, many people experience a dramatic increase in their ability to empathize with others no matter what the situation. Furthermore, it allows practitioners to listen to other viewpoints more actively, more compassionately and results in their ability to withhold judgement on thoughts and ideas that differ from their own.

4.3

While practicing mindfulness meditation might seem like a tall order at first, the truth of the matter is that being mindful is a habit which means you can learn to improve through practice, practice, practice. In fact, it should be one of the easier habits in this book to get accustomed to as it is as easy as taking a few moments out of your day to focus exclusively on the present via all of the information that your senses are bringing in.

6. *Getting started:* When you first start practicing mindfulness, it is important to always practice at the same day to ensure your body is going to get into the habit of entering a mindful state each and every day, to make the transition easier to manage. Don't forget, it takes about a month for a new habit to solidify in your mind which means that as long as you can keep it up for that amount of time you can keep it up indefinitely.

   In order to reach a state of mindfulness, you are going to want to find someplace comfortable, and quiet to sit, though not so quiet and comfortable that you are tempted to fall asleep. Then, all you need to do is breathe deeply, in and out. As you breathe in, focus all of your attention on the information that your senses are providing to you, focus on the way the air feels in your lungs, how it smells and how it tastes. Slowly but surely, expand your consciousness so that you are taking in as much information about your surroundings as possible.

7. *Observe the moment:* Mindfulness is not necessarily quieting the mind or finding an eternal state of calmness. The goal here is simple. We want to pay attention to the moment we are in without judging. When we judge a thought or something we may have done in the past, we tend to dwell on it. That isn't living in the moment and is not conducive to mindful meditation. While this is easier said than done, it is a crucial step to mindful meditation. With practice, it will be easy to achieve. Be mindful of the moment, of your senses and your surroundings.

8. *Ignore those pesky judgments:* Take notice of the times you are passing judgment while practicing. Make note of them and move on.

9. *Always come back to observation and the present moment:* It is easy for our minds to get lost in thought. Mindfulness meditation is the art of bringing yourself back to the moment, over and over, as many times as it takes. Don't get discouraged. In the beginning, you will find your mind wanders a lot. Reel it back in and keep moving forward.

10. *Be kind to yourself:* Even if your mind does happen to wander, and it will, don't be hard on yourself. It happens. Acknowledge whatever thoughts pop up, put them to the side and get back on track.

To learn more about "Declutter Your Mind" by Marie S. Davenport, visit the Amazon website.

www.ingramcontent.com/pod-product-compliance
Lightning Source LLC
Chambersburg PA
CBHW081153070526
44583CB00021B/2819